A SPECIAL
MOTHER

Other Newmarket Press Books
by Anne Ford

Laughing Allegra: The Inspiring Story of a Mother's Struggle and Triumph Raising a Daughter with Learning Disabilities

On Their Own: Creating an Independent Future for Your Adult Child with Learning Disabilities and ADHD, A Family Guide

A SPECIAL MOTHER

*Getting Through the Early Days of a
Child's Diagnosis of Learning Disabilities
and Related Disorders*

Anne Ford
with
John-Richard Thompson

Foreword by Judy Woodruff

Newmarket Press New York

This book is published in the United States of America.

First Edition

ISBN: 978-1-55704-852-3 (paperback)
ISBN: 978-1-55704-853-0 (hardcover)

10 9 8 7 6 5 4 3 2 1

Library of Congress Cataloging-in-Publication Data

Ford, Anne, 1943-
   A special mother : getting through the early days of a child's diagnosis of learning disabilities and related disorders / Anne Ford, with John-Richard Thompson ; foreword by Judy Woodruff. -- 1st ed.
       p. cm.
   Includes index.
   ISBN 978-1-55704-852-3 (pbk. : alk. paper) -- ISBN 978-1-55704-853-0 (hardcover : alk. paper) 1. Learning disabilities. 2. Learning disabled children--Family relationships. 3. Mothers of children with disabilities. I. Thompson, John-Richard. II. Title.
   RJ496.L4F67 2010
   618.92'85889--dc22
                                   2009052811

QUANTITY PURCHASES
Companies, professional groups, clubs, and other organizations may qualify for special terms when ordering quantities of this title. For information or a catalog, write Special Sales Department, Newmarket Press, 18 East 48th Street, New York, NY 10017; call (212) 832-3575 ext. 19 or 1-800-669-3903; fax (212) 832-3629; or e-mail sales@newmarketpress.com.

www.newmarketpress.com

Manufactured in the United States of America.

CONTENTS

PART III   *After the Diagnosis*

FOREWORD

JUDY WOODRUFF

W hen I sat down to write about my experiences as a mother of a son born with disabilities, I found it surprisingly difficult. First, it brought back painful memories of Jeffrey's struggles. I remembered the times he was embarrassed, and imagined similar embarrassing incidents I didn't know about. I thought also of the teachers and administrators who were so ready to write him off. But it was also difficult because I am not used to thinking about how all this affected me.

As a busy professional, I am in the habit of jumping on problems and trying to fix them. I thought I could rise to practically any challenge by planning, sheer perseverance, or, as a fallback, negotiation. My husband, with a career of his own, has the same view. Failure was not in our vocabulary, especially when it came to our children. I was much more focused on getting the desired result, surmounting the obstacle, than on my personal reactions. That was not a bad thing: it was no doubt a main reason why we were able to get through the early phase of my son's schooling.

Our son Jeffrey, now twenty-eight, was born with a mild form of spina bifida, and we had to learn a whole new way to navigate in this world.

As a young boy, Jeff was incontinent and unable to run as fast as most other boys his age. At an academically challenging school where he was practically the only child with a disability, he had to cope with diapers and bladder and bowel accidents and, eventually, being shut out of competitive athletics. He also had ill-defined learning differences. He was very bright, but began reading at a later age than many other kids, and he struggled with complex math and abstract reading assignments.

We had been alerted that Jeff might experience learning challenges, but they revealed themselves slowly. It wasn't until well into his kindergarten year that his teacher pulled us aside and said it was taking Jeff longer than most of the other kids in his class to "enjoy" books. Eventually, he got the hang of reading—became a good reader, in fact—and things smoothed out in first grade. But it wasn't long before math became an issue, and later so did his writing technique.

We were counseled to have Jeffrey independently tested, so he went through a battery of examinations, which produced a carefully worded, pessimistic report. There was no single diagnosis of a learning disability: Jeff's challenges were diffuse, as commonly happens to kids with spina bifida.

At some point, I brought to school copies of research reports I had obtained at a national spina bifida family conference, written for parents to share with their children's teachers, to help explain to them what vulnerabilities were common in these kids and some proven teaching tactics. Some instructors eagerly read the material and tried to incorporate it; others were polite but not interested. By the time Jeffrey was in the third grade, one teacher urged us to pull him out rather than face the rigors of fourth. Fortunately, the following year, Jeff's teacher was a determined woman who liked him and was prepared to do anything to make sure he learned what he needed to learn.

As I look back on the experience, it was a roller coaster: one year up, the next year down. One teacher understanding, another impatient. I can't describe my own reactions without first describing Jeffrey's: he quickly learned to hide his feelings; he became uncommonly good at acting as if none of these setbacks bothered him. He shrugged it off when learning was hard; it was no big deal. And he hated to be different from the other kids—to reveal in any way that learning was harder for him, that he needed help. In third grade, when he had to see a tutor every week, he complained that it wasn't necessary and that he was being unfairly singled out.

I had a hard time accepting that Jeff's learning problems were a permanent condition. I very much wanted to believe these were issues that could be overcome by hard work or tutoring. When I finally absorbed the fact that my beloved, adorable son was facing a long stretch of not only hard work, but harder work than most of his peers, it hurt. It hurt even more whenever he was singled out for his differences. It broke my heart. Not as much as it would be broken years later when Jeffrey experienced a serious health setback, but it was a definable ache that ebbed and flowed depending on how easy or hard a particular week went.

He managed to do well in school, with the help of tutors and other experts. But my husband and I often felt alone, navigating in unchartered waters, with few other boats. As far as we knew, few if any other kids and parents were going through anything similar. The school was focused on diversity of socioeconomic background and athletic ability, but not of learning styles. I didn't know many other mothers I felt comfortable sharing our worries and fears with.

That's why this book is so valuable. Anne Ford has been a tireless advocate for children with learning disabilities. In *A Special Mother* she tells her own story and the stories of other mothers who might never have known about each other and might have assumed, as I did, that their situation was unique. If, in the earliest stages of understanding our child has a learning disability, we are able to recognize the signs, ask the right questions, seek help in the right places, we—and our children—might be spared some of the inevitable pain of this diagnosis.

One of the things we now know about learning disabilities is that they affect not just the child but the child's family as well, often the mother most directly. You are fortunate to be reading this book, a supportive road map for the journey that lies ahead.

Judy Woodruff is a well-known news anchor and journalist.

Note to Readers

We are pleased to announce that we have partnered with the National Center for Learning Disabilities (NCLD) to create a Web site component dedicated to the issues raised in this book. There's a lot of great information out there on learning disabilities, more than we could possibly include in a single book. Through our link to NCLD's Web site at www.ld.org/aspecialmother, you will find links to further information, worksheets, resources, and other topics we could not include here. For example, I mention Parent Training and Information Centers (PTI) in the book. The Web site gives you more information about these centers and guides you to a state-by-state directory of them. To read about other topics beyond the confines of this book, go to the main NCLD Web site, www.ld.org, for links to excerpts from my previous books, *Laughing Allegra* and *On Their Own*, and to a wealth of further information and advice. These Web sites are updated from time to time, so you can always be assured of receiving the very latest news and information.

Both this book and the Web page were created to provide a basic understanding of the issues involved with a diagnosis of LD or a related disorder. They do not constitute legal advice and should not be used as a legal resource.

Introduction
Special Mothers

M y first book, *Laughing Allegra*, was a memoir of raising a daughter born with severe learning disabilities and how that experience affected and shaped our family. I called it a "guide to the heart" in the hope of touching parents who faced a similar situation. My second book, *On Their Own*, continued the story as my daughter entered adulthood by focusing on the challenges common to most adults with learning disabilities, or LD, as they embark on an independent life. With *A Special Mother*, I return to the early years of a child's initial diagnosis with LD and related disorders and focus on the person who stands at the center of it all: the mother.

I have many reasons for writing this book, but the main one is this: I want to praise our heroes—mothers, *all* mothers. When our children are born, we are the first to hold them, the first to feed them, the first to cuddle them and to give them love. We hover over their cribs at night and watch them sleep, we listen to their every breath, we watch them grow, we marvel at their first word and cry a little at their first step. We create scrapbooks that chronicle their young lives. We make imprints of their hands and feet and proudly display their childish artwork on the art gallery we call "the refrigerator." We travel hand in hand through all they encounter in an effort to give them the best lives possible.

We mothers are all so different. Some hold down two jobs while raising a family. Some work full-time as a mother in the home. Some are married, some are single. Some have children of their own and some have stepchildren. No matter which category we fall into, mothers tend to become the engine that pulls the family train. Sometimes it happens that one of the cars in that train does not roll along as smoothly as the others. There may be a diagnosis of a learning disability or related disorder that slows things down a bit, but that does not stop the engine. The effort may be a little harder now, but on we go; and it is this single-minded advocacy I hope to both praise and inspire.

The second reason for writing the book is to pass on this advice as strenuously as I can: when you get the results of the first diagnosis of LD, Asperger's Syndrome, anxiety disorder, or any similar disability, do not panic. Get a second opinion. More important, understand and believe that you truly do have the ability to enable your child to succeed. The trick is not to give in to despair. Yes, you will have days when you feel you can do little more than sit down and cry your heart out. I did many times. I have yet to meet a mother of a child with LD who hasn't. Sometimes the challenges seem insurmountable, the obstacles too high, the lows too deep; but that will pass. Even the truly impossible challenges will pass. You'll simply find a way around them or through them or over them.

I always say that the two happiest days of my life were the day my son was born, in 1966, and my daughter was born, in 1972. I'm sure every mother feels the same about the birth of her children. The labor is long and hard, but the reward at the end is beyond words, almost beyond imagining. We are so happy when the pediatrician checks our baby out and everything seems perfect, so why would we ever imagine that there might be a "problem" with this perfect baby—especially if the problem turns out to be one we cannot see, such as a learning disability?

We are blindsided by these disorders. They seem to come out of the blue, and most of us are unprepared to handle them. Even those we might think are the best prepared—someone in the medical community, for example, or a professional educator—may be at a loss when their own child is diagnosed with a learning disability. Panic-stricken, bewildered and confused, lost, overwhelmed, sorrowful: these are a few of the words mothers use when talking about the experience. Some feel they can never be fully happy again, for they see only struggles and problems ahead for their child and take the saying to be true: they can only be as happy as their least happy child.

One of the most peculiar, yet universal, traits found in all mothers of children with LD or related disabilities is the feeling that we're completely alone in this, as if no one before us has ever experienced similar emotions, and no one around us could possibly understand what we are going through.

I was certainly like that. "No one," I thought, "absolutely *no one* I know has ever gone through this—no family members, no friends, not even casual acquaintances." The irony is that, today, hardly a day goes by when I don't meet someone who knows exactly what it's like to have a child, family member, or friend who has LD.

It can happen anywhere.

In Michigan, a lovely woman who drove me from the airport to a hotel spent half of the drive telling me of her troubles with her daughter who has severe ADHD.

In California, I visited a vineyard where a woman pulled me aside to tell me about her son's lifelong difficulties with dyslexia.

In New York, on the street, in a restaurant, in a bookstore—no matter where I am, the moment someone hears that I have written a book about LD, or have a daughter with LD, the floodgates open and I find that I am far from alone in my experience.

Mothers of children with LD are not the only ones who talk to me. Mothers experiencing any problem with their children, from anxiety disorder to autism and even alcohol or substance abuse, reach out when they sense a kindred spirit. Similar threads of anxiety and fear are woven through them all.

Another trait I have found is genuine, heartfelt pain, demonstrated mostly by the quivering voice and the welling of tears in the eyes, which sometimes break free and flow down the cheeks, while the voice cracks. This is not always the pain of something the mother is experiencing at that moment. It is often old pain, from an old wound that has never healed. It is the pain of remembering night after night of trying to sleep, tossing and turning, wondering if you did the right thing, or didn't do the right thing, and what you should do now. It is the pain of feeling absolutely helpless, of not knowing where to turn or who to turn to, and feeling for certain that whatever turn you make will not be the right one, and wondering if you will ever be able to do exactly the right thing.

Worst of all is the feeling that you have no way of knowing

whether your fears are unfounded. You don't know if what you are worried about one particular day or week or month is something truly serious, or if it is a small matter that will clear up on its own. That's how it can be with LD: we're confronted with a host of bewildering problems and find it extremely difficult to sort them based on order of importance. I have met some mothers who cry so hard they can barely talk. When I finally get the story out of them, I summon a knowing smile because I faced the exact same dilemma and well remember the sense that the sky was falling.

Sometimes those horrible problems turn out to be not much of a problem at all. Other times the sense of fear and panic is warranted. It's very difficult to tell which it might be when you're in the middle of it all, with no opportunity or ability to step back and calmly evaluate the situation. This type of mother often seeks reassurance, but chances are, she has no interest in hearing someone tell her, "It's not that bad." For her, it *is* that bad.

One mother I spoke with for this book said, "Having a child is like having a string tied to your heart. You can always feel it…when that child is out in the world, you can still feel it. It gets strained sometimes, but it never breaks. That string never leaves you."

I feel the same way. I have had strings attached to my heart since the day my son, Alessandro, was born. My two children are the source of my greatest joy; but there is no question that they came with a minor price. In my case (and I suspect many, many others) that price is worry.

Oh, my goodness…worry. I've talked about it in my two previous books, I talk about it whenever I speak to groups of mothers, I think about it all the time because it is always, always present in my life. With Alessandro, the worry always took the standard, mothering type of worry. With Allegra, born with multiple learning disabilities, the worry took a more uncertain, insidious turn: "What is going to happen to her?"; "What if she can't go to school?"; "What if she has no friends?"; and worst of all, "What will happen to her after I'm gone?"

Worries are always with me. Some fell by the wayside as Allegra grew into a happy, vibrant adult with many friends. Some will never go away, though they have lessened over time. And some, the deepest ones, seem to hang around and trouble me long after they should have been laid to rest.

"Was it my fault?"

"Did I make the right decisions for her?"

"Should I have let her move away from home so soon?" (The answer to this is a resounding "Yes!" Learning to *let go* was the most important step I took in the quest for Allegra's independence.)

In spite of the occasional specific question, much of my worry is absolutely generic and based on nothing at all. I will wake up and suddenly think, *for no reason*, "Something is going to happen to her today." I never think that about Alessandro. I only think it about Allegra, as if all the fears and confusions from the earliest years of her diagnosis never fully left me but remain inside, lurking below the surface, ready to pounce at unexpected moments.

Recently, a friend traveling with me casually asked why I don't put my cell phone on silent before I go to sleep. Without thinking, I said, "Because Allegra couldn't talk to me if I did that."

"Well, yes," she said, "but even if she could contact you...what could you do? You're here. She's there. It's the middle of the night. What can you possibly do before tomorrow morning?"

It's not logical, and I know it's not, but that doesn't matter. "I know I can't do anything right now," I said, "but the very first thing I ask myself whenever I travel is 'how quickly can I get home if I have to?'" I have traveled to some far-flung places in the last years, and I would have had a great deal of trouble getting home quickly; but that's okay. It gave me something to worry about, and I seem to need that.

Allegra is thirty-seven years old, but I remain as worried, diligent, and watchful as the mother of a teenager who has taken the car out for the first time.

These generic worries and fears remain with me, but none can compare to the early days of Allegra's diagnosis. I suspect it is the same for most mothers. Some have sons and daughters who are now approaching middle age, yet these mothers are still so scarred by those early traumas that they can recount them in great detail, and with the same emotions they experienced twenty or thirty years before.

Other mothers are experiencing those traumas now. Maybe you

are one of them, reading this book, trying to find a way out of this trouble you have quite unexpectedly found in your life. My friend Christina Giamalva described it to me this way: "It's like I was driving along the highway, and suddenly somebody put a gun to my head and forced me onto a dark, lonely road."

Was it like that for you? With no signs, no guideposts, nothing familiar or comforting, and seemingly no safe exit and no companion who truly understands and can help you on this frightening journey?

My hope is that this book will become that companion. I may not have experienced the exact same situation you face now, but chances are good that I have experienced similar feelings. I hope to reach down to where your emotions reside, in those secret, hurt places that you feel may never truly heal. Yes, I know you are looking for hard information, and you will find it here—but I know you are also looking for some comfort and some sense that others out there understand what you are going through.

In the following pages you will hear from experts, but also from mothers, real mothers who told me their stories and who have become members of what I call the "Special Mothers Club": Helen, Janie, Dana, Lisa, and Deborah. I've known Deborah for many years. Her daughter Windy was a classmate of Allegra's at the Riverview School on Cape Cod. The others I met through a friend. They all have younger children and, coincidentally, all have boys with LD, whereas Deborah and I have daughters with LD. We all got together at Helen's house in a small, leafy village north of Boston. One mother, Dana, has a son with anxiety disorder. This is not a specific learning disability, but as you'll see, LD is often accompanied by related disorders such as ADHD or anxiety disorder. I find that the experiences and emotions of these mothers are nearly interchangeable, regardless of whether their child has LD or one of the related disorders, and that is what I want to focus on: the commonality of our emotions, not the specifics of our child's disability.

These mothers' stories are interspersed throughout the book, their experiences and insight illuminating a path through the darkness. Theirs is an emotional story, for LD—if nothing else—is an emotional issue. We can focus on facts, figures, charts, and graphs all we want, but sooner or later, without fail, we will find ourselves bogged down in feelings that cannot be relieved by reading cold statistics.

The members of the Special Mothers Club had never talked about the emotional side of LD before. They had lots of experience with school groups in which they discussed school-related issues, but never before had they sat down over coffee and talked about the things that most kept them up at night with worry and even panic. It has proved to be very therapeutic for them. Dana put it this way: "I saw Janie at school the other day...and the only way I know her is from those times we got together to talk about these things. We waved to each other and smiled. I know she is out there now, and I know she is going through this, too. And, most important, I know that we're all going to be okay."

There is something else you will find here. You may not actively seek it out, but you deserve it all the same, and that is acknowledgment of your own heroism, for you *are* a hero (or, more properly, a heroine). We all are. We have obligations, we have duties and responsibilities that tie us down and keep us awake at night, and rarely do we get credit for fulfilling them. And why should we? We only do what those strings attached to our hearts compel us to do. Even so, when a child with a disability of any kind enters the family, the pressures increase, the sense of responsibility increases, and fear and doubt sometimes threaten to overwhelm. That is why it is important now and then to take a moment to give yourself credit for being what you are: an engine that may falter at times, but does not fail. A hero. A Special Mother.

PART I

Before the Diagnosis

Chapter 1

"Something's Not Quite Right": The Role of Mother's Intuition

"We were in the car, driving to get ice cream," Helen remembers. "It was a perfectly ordinary day, nothing special at all. My husband, Jim, was driving, I was in the front seat beside him. Our son, Michael, and our daughter, Emma, were in the back, along with Sarah, one of Emma's friends. Michael was about five then, and Emma and Sarah were about three and a half. They were talking away and laughing in the backseat, and I was only half paying attention. They made up a rhyming game, where one would say a word and someone else had to say another word that rhymed.

"'Dog,' Sarah said, and without a moment's hesitation, my daughter, Emma, said, 'Log.' She thought for a second and then came up with a new word: 'Cow.'

"'Now,' said Sarah, and then she rhymed two words on her own. 'Sarah—Tara.' Emma caught on and did the same: 'Emma—Temma.' It didn't make sense; they were only three and half. And then Michael, a year and a half older than the two girls, chimed in with a rhyme of his own.

"'Dog—Cow!' he said, and the girls laughed.

"I laughed, too. 'He's always making jokes,' I thought to myself with a smile.

"'That doesn't rhyme!' Emma cried, and Michael—in all seriousness—said, 'Yes, it does.'

3

"*Click*.

"Something fell into place in my mind and deep within my heart...I *knew* Michael wasn't joking. I knew he couldn't tell whether *Dog* and *Cow* rhymed or did not rhyme. I looked at my husband. He gazed at the road ahead. He hadn't noticed. I didn't say anything, but sat back and turned my head to the side, listening.

"'Tree—Me,' the girls said; 'House—Mouse'; and then Michael tried to do the same: 'Bridge—Road.' Again the girls laughed and told him he did it wrong.

"'No, I didn't!' Michael said.

"This time Jim heard it, too. We exchanged a quick glance. He raised his eyebrows and then returned to his own thoughts and the road ahead.

"He was able to do that. I could not. I couldn't return to whatever I had been thinking before the rhyming game. The whole way to the ice cream shop and back home, I couldn't seem to rid my mind of the question, *Why?*

"*Why* couldn't he rhyme? It was obvious how to do it, so *why* couldn't he do it? The girls are almost two years younger; *why* could they do it but he couldn't?

"Later that evening I asked my husband if he heard it.

"'Heard what?' he asked.

"'Michael. He couldn't rhyme like the girls.'

"'Oh, yeah. I guess I heard it...but so what?'

"'But *why*?' I asked. 'Doesn't it seem strange? He's older than both girls, he should be able to do that.'

"'He can do it,' Jim insisted. 'He didn't feel like playing, or maybe he was making a joke—you know how he is. Or maybe he was thinking about something else. It's nothing....'

"I wasn't so sure," Helen says. "I felt that it might be a sign of something, but I had no idea what that something might be."

IS IT ME?

That strange, mystical thing we call Mother's Intuition is rarely the final word on whether or not a child has a learning disability, but in many cases, it is the first word.

Mothers, like Helen, who eventually find themselves entangled in the maze of evaluations, school meetings, and the confusing world of Special Education can usually look back and pinpoint the moment when it all started, when something deep inside whispered, "Something's not quite right."

"That little episode with the rhyming in the backseat was the first hint of trouble ahead," Helen says. "Jim couldn't see it. He thought I was crazy, worrying too much, imagining things…but I couldn't shake the feeling that something wasn't quite right. And the thing is, the important thing is, I would never have thought twice about it if I hadn't been able to compare him to Emma. I didn't know whether or not Michael should be able to rhyme at five years old. He was my first child—I didn't know every developmental milestone by heart. But when your daughter who is a year and a half younger can rhyme and your son can't…well, that was something that caught my attention. I was on the lookout from that moment on."

That's how it starts, a nagging feeling that something isn't quite right, as if the ground beneath you has shifted slightly. It is only a small disorientation at this point. You haven't stepped in the quicksand yet; you don't feel anything close to the sinking, helpless sensations that come later, but still…*something's not quite right.*

Helen's situation was far from unusual. Here is Janie, another member of our Special Mothers Club. We sat around a table, all six of us, to discuss the various issues related to LD. I had asked when they first suspected something might be wrong.

"I have a son named Mark," Janie told me. "He's nine now, but I first noticed something different about him when he was not quite two years old. I just could not get him out of the house. It was nearly impossible to get him organized enough to leave the house. Little things like getting his shoes on or his coat on were so difficult. I'd get one shoe on, and then couldn't find the other one, and when I did, the first shoe would be off again. 'Mark, go get your coat and scarf,' I'd say. He'd get his scarf but couldn't find his coat, and then his shoes would be off again. It was like that every single morning. Everything was so *difficult.* He didn't have any siblings at that time—he was my first child, so I thought it was normal behavior. But then I saw other children and other mothers, and I thought, 'Why can't I do that? What's wrong with *me*?' I blamed myself.

"At that point, it never occurred to me that there might be something wrong with Mark. It *had* to be me, I thought. When he was two I had my second child, but I still didn't see anything wrong with Mark. I put all the blame on myself. Everything was difficult. Everything! Bedtime was difficult. He wouldn't sit still when I tried to read him a story. Feeding was difficult. Everything was a task. When he was four, we started going to Kindermusic, a music program for kindergarten children. The kids would have to go to their bag, get their music book, and sit down. Simple, right? But Mark would go to the bag and draw a blank, as if he was thinking, 'What do I do next?' And the teacher always had to follow him to make sure he was doing what she asked. She didn't follow the other children, only him. But for some reason I still thought it seemed normal. I guess I didn't really notice all the effort she had to put into it, but then things started to get worse. Eventually the teacher said, 'Do you think there's a disability here?' That was how she said it.

"I was shocked! I couldn't even answer. I still thought everything was going the way it was supposed to, and if Mark was a little scattered and disorganized it was because *I* was doing something wrong—not him. The teacher said, 'He's fed the information, but'—she pointed to her head—'he just can't get it up here.' I don't think I really heard what she said. I focused more on the *way* she said it. 'Why would anyone say that?!' I thought to myself. I became defensive, and thought, 'Who the heck are you to say something to me about my four-year-old kid?'

"I thought those things, but I didn't say them out loud. I think I probably muttered, 'No, there's nothing wrong,' or something like that, and left with Mark. But the truth is, that was the first time anyone said anything about a disability of any kind, and even though I didn't respond, I started to watch more closely. I thought, 'Okay, let me prove she's wrong. Let's see if he can do this one time.' So I said, 'Mark, go get your shoes, brush your teeth, and meet me at the front door.' This time I watched, and I could see that even that simple combination of tasks was beyond him. He would start off fine and then stop and say, 'What did you want me to do?' It would eventually get done, but it became so frustrating for me, all the questions, all the stops and starts, and I would get angry and say, 'Your brother just did it and he's only two—what's your *problem?*'

"Mark would get as frustrated as me. I gave him a bad rap, I really did. I started to think he was just being a pain, or he was just a bad kid. But I knew in my heart that he wasn't bad. He couldn't stay focused. He couldn't follow through on directions. He then went into kindergarten, and once again he had trouble. Just learning to put his backpack on, or stand in line, or take his seat was difficult—and that's without the academics. He couldn't do it all. He was trying to remember, 'Okay, I have to do this, and then that, and then this,' and that was all before he sat down in class. Forget about the alphabet! Truthfully, I don't know how he got through it. And then came first grade and all his spelling words came back wrong. Unless I drilled something into him—*drilled* it—he couldn't retain it. Eventually, he was diagnosed with a broad spectrum of processing disorders, mostly auditory processing problems, but that evaluation didn't come until later."

Sometimes a mother will not be the first to see anything wrong or, if she does, she misinterprets it as something else, such as poor behavior or slow development. Often, as in Janie's case, she will put the blame on herself. "I'm a bad mother," she may think, or "What am I doing wrong?" But even then, once the problem is pointed out, this mother may look at the situation in a new light: all the various elements will click together and she will say, "Oh yes, so *that's* what all of that meant."

SPOTTING A PROBLEM EARLY

Lisa, another mother at the table, says that she knew something was wrong the day her son, Ryan, was born.

"How did you know that?" I asked.

"Mother's Intuition," she said. "It had to be Mother's Intuition because I didn't really have any practical experience or knowledge apart from what I read in books. I was the first of my group of friends to get married, the first to have a child, and I was the baby of the family, so I didn't have a lot of experience with babies. But I'm a big researcher, so I read every book I could find. I was so excited; but when he was born he was nothing like the baby I read about in all those books. For one thing, he never stopped crying. Never! He suffered dehydration because he couldn't eat anything. The doctor said he was a colicky baby. The only time he stopped crying was if I held him close and took him into the shower. I had to hold him, and I stood there until the water ran cold. He also got ear infections every month for the first two years of his life. He was allergic to penicillin and sulfa drugs, so he couldn't take anything...I got so attuned that I could smell the ear infection a week before the doctor could locate it. His ear would get a certain smell—and I would hold him, and I would smell his ear, and I knew it was coming again. He didn't sleep through the night until he was three. It was a complete nightmare. And to top it all off, he never spoke. Some of my relatives called him 'The Velcro Kid' because he was so clingy. Later, the doctors discovered he was partially deaf because of the constant ear infections. They inserted tubes in his ears, and that rectified that, but as a result he had a delay in speech.

"I then had a second child, my daughter, Emily, who was a dream and a doll, and everything I read about in those books. And like Janie said earlier, watching a younger sibling with no problem reinforced the idea that something wasn't quite right with Ryan. Like Janie, I, too, had trouble getting him dressed. I couldn't get him out of the house. He couldn't get his shoes on, or his jacket, or he couldn't find something he needed. We would visit some of my friends who had children the same age as Ryan, and everything seemed effortless to them."

"That's exactly what happened to me!" Janie interjected. "It made me feel terrible about myself."

"Me, too!" Lisa said. "I would think, 'Oh, my God, I must be the worst mom in the world!' It takes me forty-five minutes to get out the door...he can't find his shoe, he puts on his coat the wrong way, he's got two different-colored socks on...and then by the time I've left the house, I've missed the appointment."

LISTEN TO YOUR INTUITION

Our intuition is present whether we want it or not, whether we understand its meaning or not. Some of us would have been happy to be oblivious to it, for much of what we intuit revolves around our deepest, most negative fears. Few mothers say their intuition led them to secretly believe their preschool child was showing signs of becoming a nuclear physicist. It's usually a feeling that we have suddenly veered off course…just a little, perhaps…but the path we thought was straight and true has suddenly developed a few unexpected curves.

Some mothers suppress that intuitive voice. They ignore it, or push it down and away, until it cannot make itself heard. Why would they do that? Isn't it better to face the problem squarely and honestly? Maybe so, but it isn't always easy, especially since we are often the first and only ones who feel these things (we don't often hear about Father's Intuition, after all, or Sister-in-Law's Intuition). You have others arrayed against you who will insist you are imagining things, or that it means nothing, or it's not as bad as you suspect.

What a relief, you think. It's me. *I* am the problem! I worry too much. It's normal; my child will grow into it. If I just ignore it, the whole thing will go away.

Lisa puts it this way: "When you have that first child, you invest so much in the *idea* of a child. It's a blessing, it's the best thing that has ever happened to you, and as a woman, it's all about the investment. I ate right, I have my education, I have a stable marriage, I did all the right things. The equation says your child should be fine, and when that child is not fine, you feel shortchanged. You say, 'But I invested, and I did the work'…and you have to realize you don't have that control. It's all a matter of letting go of that control. As a parent, you get such a sense of power. We control everything. We control when our kids eat, when they sleep, what schools they go to, what their room looks like, what their religion is going to be, what moral values they will have…but you can't control learning disabilities.

"LD is an affront to our position of power. Parents either learn how to work with it and be flexible or they become more rigid and fight back. You have to realize that perhaps your child is not going to grow up and become a doctor in the traditional way. It may not be what is meant for your child. But if you're like me, you'll come to realize that if your child is meant to become a doctor, it is going to be arduous and more likely require a different path to get there. I have learned so much from my son. Maybe the most important thing I've learned is that there is no perfect way to get anywhere."

Our dreams and assumptions can be a stumbling block to acceptance. I myself had built up such a rosy future for my daughter, Allegra, that I simply could not face any sort of threat to that future. By this I don't mean that I actively ignored things I saw, but that I truly did not see them. My walls of denial were so strong and had been built so high that I had to be forcibly shown the truth before I could begin to accept it. I certainly had Mother's Intuition. As mothers, I'm not sure we can avoid it. I had moments of thinking, "Hmmm...something's not quite right," but I never for a moment connected her actions with a disability of any kind. My daughter was unfocused and had trouble paying attention, "but so what?" I thought. "She has too much energy, she is a free spirit, she does things her own way, she will settle down eventually."

I wanted so much for there to be nothing wrong that I managed to will myself into believing that there wasn't. This did me no good at all, as I couldn't hold reality at bay forever.

Most have an experience similar to another of our mothers, Deborah, who said, "When I was pregnant with our daughter Windy, I really tried to take care of myself. I wanted to give this child a very healthy start, and so in delivery, I tried not to take any medication. Everything went fine, and our daughter was a beautiful baby. She had a sparkle and she was filled with joy. All that is still with her, but I began to sense that something wasn't quite right when she was about two. She was our first child, so I couldn't compare her to another child, but I just *knew*. There wasn't anything wrong with her as far as her physical aspects were concerned. She was highly verbal, too, so that didn't raise any alarm bells, but I noticed a problem with her hand-eye coordination."

"How did you notice that?" I asked. "Did you compare her to another child?"

Deborah paused for a moment, as if unsure of her answer. "No," she finally said. "I don't know how I knew. There was just something about her that I could see and no one else seemed to notice."

When these feelings first arise, most mothers do not immediately think of a learning disability. *Immaturity* is usually the first word that comes to mind, or a delay in development, and the fact is, they may be right (in this very early stage, it is extremely difficult to tell the difference between LD and delays in development). The important thing is to *trust* your instincts and *accept* your instincts. Don't turn away from them. Monitor your child closely.

Professionals rely on the mother for much of the information used to evaluate a child, so don't be afraid to talk about your concerns with your child's pediatrician. Don't fall into the trap of thinking, "Oh, so what if he can't rhyme words as well as the other children? It's not important."

Those first rumblings and hints there might be trouble ahead are not easy to deal with, regardless of whether you panic easily or are as smooth as silk. You are bound to feel a tightness in the stomach and a sinking feeling that things are not what they should be or seemed to be only weeks or months before. No one wants to admit her child may have trouble learning. We don't want him or her to be "labeled" as having a disability of any kind, especially one that, on the surface, gets so tangled up with normal delays in development that we truly don't know if there is a problem or not.

The trick is to *pay attention*. Flying into a panic won't help, nor will pushing your concerns onto a back burner. Many teachers will advise a wait-and-see approach, and sometimes that is sound advice. Wait and see...but not for long! Keep a close and careful watch, and if something more shows itself or if someone else brings a problem to your attention, be prepared to act on it.

You should also prepare yourself for resistance when first bringing your fears to someone else's attention. Your husband, for example, may tell you it's all in your mind and there's nothing wrong at all. The pediatrician may say (or, at least, think) the same thing, and guess what— they are right! It *is* in your mind. Your intuition is the strongest and most effective tool you have at this stage of the game. Trust it. Try to push denial and your fears to the side. You truly do know more about your child than you think you know, and if you feel strongly that something isn't quite right, don't turn away from those feelings based on something someone else tells you or on the misguided hope that if you don't acknowledge the problem, it will go away.

Keep watching.

Let your intuition be your guide.

It may not give you firm answers, but it will certainly tell you that you *need* answers.

"Well, that's fine," you say. "But what am I supposed to look for?"

Chapter 2
"Why Can't She Get It?":
Understanding Learning
Disabilities

F ew of us come to motherhood prepared with a Master's degree in Child Development with a special emphasis on Learning Disorders. Most of us know next to nothing about LD before our families become immersed in the issue. The general public's knowledge and understanding of LD can best be summed up by this statement: "Oh, right, dyslexia…that's reversing letters or something like that, isn't it?"

Back when I started my journey with LD, we did not have the easy access to information available to the mothers of today. But easy access to information is one thing; making sense of it all is quite another. I had no end of questions, but I was afraid to ask most of them. "My questions are too dumb," I thought, "or they're unanswerable." Some mothers think their questions are too trivial and don't want to bother anyone with their concerns.

Nonsense! No question is too trivial or unintelligent when it comes to your child. Some of your questions might be unanswerable, but that doesn't mean they shouldn't be asked.

This chapter will ask and answer the most common questions, starting with the most basic (and sometimes most difficult) of all.

WHAT IS A LEARNING DISABILITY?

I raised a daughter born with severe LD, I spent twelve years as chairman of the National Center for Learning Disabilities, I have written three books on the subject, and still this is the question I often find most daunting. There are easy definitions, of course, but LD itself can be very complicated.

In Allegra's case, her disabilities are so varied and cover so much territory that I am always at a loss to explain them fully, even to myself. When she was a child, I couldn't understand how she could be a competitive figure skater and yet not know her right from her left. Such questions persist long after she's become an adult. How, for instance, can she plan and host a perfect dinner party for six guests, yet the following night have trouble reading the menu in a restaurant? These specific questions have no concrete explanation, but certainly some questions about LD are answerable.

Here is what we know. A learning disability is a neurological disorder. In other words, it results from a difference in the way a person's brain is "wired." A learning disability means that a person of at least average intelligence will have difficulty acquiring basic academic skills, skills that are essential for success at school and for coping with life in general. "Why can't she *get* it?" is the phrase a mother may conjure in her mind during a homework session, or "Why can't he *see* that is not the right answer?" when she looks over a quiz her son has brought home with yet another D scrawled at the top.

Children with LD may be as smart or smarter than their peers, but they may have difficulty reading, writing, spelling, reasoning, recalling, and/or organizing information if they are taught in conventional ways.

DO LEARNING DISABILITIES INVOLVE ONLY ACADEMICS?

Oh, if only that were the case! Most of us could far more easily deal with LD and its consequences if they were confined to the classroom. Yes, it would be difficult, and we would be distressed to see our child struggle in school; but some of the most gut-wrenching emotions associated with LD come as a result of a child's difficulties with social skills and lack of friends. Not all children with LD have these problems, but enough of them do that it becomes a major—sometimes the major—concern for mothers. Rick Lavoie, the former headmaster of one of

Allegra's schools, says, "No parent ever comes to my office crying about low math scores. It is the lack of friends that breaks a mother's heart."

I'll talk about problems with social skills in chapter 19.

IS THERE A CURE FOR LD?

LD is not a disease whose cure awaits a miracle drug as yet undiscovered in the rainforest. There is no cure. LD is a lifelong issue. With the right support and intervention, however, children with LD can succeed in school and go on to successful, often distinguished careers later in life.

Mothers can help by encouraging their child's strengths, knowing their child's weaknesses, understanding the educational system, working with professionals, and learning about strategies for dealing with LD—all subjects we will touch upon further in this book.

WHAT ARE THE TYPES OF LEARNING DISABILITIES?

Learning disabilities come in myriad forms and degrees, and the terminology used to define them seems to expand and become more complicated year by year. As no two children are alike, so, too, can we say that no two learning disabilities are alike. Broadly speaking, we can categorize them as follows:

Reading, or Dyslexia. This is not simply a matter of reversing letters. *Dyslexia* refers to all reading-based disabilities, in which a person has trouble understanding written words.

Math, or Dyscalculia. An inability to solve arithmetic problems or grasp math concepts.

Writing, or Dysgraphia. A writing disability in which a person finds it difficult to form letters or write within a defined space.

Listening and Speaking, or Auditory and Visual Processing Disorders. A person with these sensory disabilities has difficulty understanding language despite normal hearing and vision.

Nonverbal Learning Disabilities. The term *nonverbal LD* is a little confusing. Among researchers, there is still no firm agreement about what, exactly, the term means and it isn't always accepted by educators and other professionals as a distinct disorder. In general, nonverbal LD means an inability to process information that is not verbal or language-based. This includes problems with visual-spatial perceptions, problems interpreting facial cues, difficulties with social skills, talking but saying very little, or focusing on details without being able to see the big picture.

Your child may fit into one, some, or all of these categories. Only an evaluation can say for sure.

IS LD THE SAME AS AUTISM OR ASPERGER'S SYNDROME?

No. Ten or so years ago there used to be thick bright boundary lines between LD and various disorders, such as autism and Asperger's, but I've noticed a shift in the professional thinking. It is no longer taboo or even unusual to hear LD and Asperger's spoken of in the same sentence (though autism is still considered a completely different disorder).

Although Asperger's Syndrome is not the same as autism, it is in the same "family" of autism spectrum disorders that are characterized by difficulties with social relations and repetitive patterns of behavior. Although Asperger's may affect learning, it is not considered a learning disability. LD is not an autism spectrum disorder. Children with Asperger's most often have their greatest difficulties interacting socially with their peers. They may also have unusual or elaborate preoccupations with objects or topics.

WHAT ARE SOME OF THE "RELATED DISORDERS" THAT OFTEN GO ALONG WITH LD?

In Dr. Larry Silver's article "Are Learning Disabilities the Only Problem? You Should Know About Other Related Disorders," he explains that about half the people with LD have one or more related disorders as well.

These related disorders include:

- **Attention Deficit/Hyperactivity Disorder (ADHD)**

  This may be the related disorder that is most often associated with LD (some experts believe it happens as often as 40 percent of the time). ADHD is not a learning disability (children without LD can certainly have ADHD), but it often goes hand in hand with a diagnosis of LD.

- **Regulation of Emotions**

  Dr. Silver includes a group of disorders under this broad heading. "For most people with LD," he writes, "the problems of regulating their emotions are not situational—they are neurologically based. The problems have a chronic history, often beginning in early childhood, and are pervasive, occurring at home, in school, with friends and during all months of the year. Often there is a family history of similar problems."

  These types of emotional or psychological-related problems include:

  Anxiety Disorders. These might be related to specific situations, such as separation, social interactions, performance, specific objects, or specific places, or the anxiety disorder might be generalized to most aspects of life.

  Depression. Behaviors suggesting depression might include an irritable mood, decreased interest or loss of pleasure in many activities, sleep disturbances, and decreased ability to concentrate.

  Anger Control. This behavior goes beyond a typical tantrum. Problems with anger control lead to real "meltdowns." The child will quickly lose his or her temper, often so fast that it is not clear what set it off. The episode can last for five or ten minutes, or up to an hour, and end as quickly as it began. Once over, the child may feel sorry for the behavior and have difficulty explaining it.

Obsessive-Compulsive Disorder.

These problems often begin in early childhood. Some children might have difficulty with obsessive thoughts. Others might have the need to carry out compulsive behaviors. Others will have both problems.

• Other Brain-Processing Disorders

Many people with LD will also have a Language Disability, a Motor Coordination Disorder, or problems with Organization and Executive Function (problems organizing materials and losing, forgetting, or misplacing things).

• Tic Disorders

Some children with LD may have trouble regulating certain motor functions. Contractions of muscles can cause motor tics. Others have oral tics: they feel the need to say certain sounds or words.

• Bipolar Disorder

The main behavior pattern with bipolar disorder relates to mood swings, usually from depression to extreme happiness, referred to as manic behavior.

For more information and a fuller description of all these related disorders, read Dr. Silver's entire article online (www.ldonline.org). You can also find a wealth of information in his book *The Misunderstood Child*.

HOW CAN I TELL IF MY PRESCHOOL-AGED SON HAS LD OR IF HE IS DEVELOPMENTALLY DELAYED?

This is such a difficult question that I am inclined to say, "You can't tell the difference—at least, not at first." This is what makes Early Identification so difficult, and yet so important. I will explore this topic further in the following chapter, but for now, let's look at some of the broad differences between typical and atypical development in early childhood, as defined by the National Center for Learning Disabilities.

Typical

Children gather information from people, things, and events in their environment. They then organize this information in their minds in ways that keep it usable and easily understood. They do this by matching the information with what they've learned before, noticing similarities and differences, and storing the information for future use. Once they have done this, they will behave in ways that suggest that learning has taken place. (For example, once a child learns how to make the letter A, he or she will be able to recognize that letter in a word.) A child's development will usually follow a known and predictable course, and the acquisition of certain skills and abilities is often used to gauge children's development.

These skills and abilities are known as *developmental milestones* and include such things as crawling, walking, saying single words, putting words together into phrases and sentences, and following directions. (You will find information about developmental milestones on NCLD's *A Special Mother* Web page at www.ld.org/aspecialmother).

It is important to remember that not all children reach each milestone at the same time. Some children may be very advanced in their use of oral language at an age when others are just discovering the power of spoken words. Some children may be advanced in motor skills, while others are reluctant to use certain toys or engage in building activities or crafts projects.

Growth patterns within different children can also vary. Children who show strength in one area of development might be slower to develop skills in another. For example, a child who has a wonderful ability to understand spoken language might struggle with verbal expression.

These all fall within what is considered typical development.

Atypical

Some children exhibit behaviors that fall outside the normal, or expected, range of development. These behaviors emerge in a way or at a pace that is different from that of their peers. It is important for parents to watch carefully to determine whether the behavior is a reflection of the child's unique personality or whether it shows an area of weakness and concern.

Atypical behaviors should be noted and carefully recorded. They may be isolated events that have little or no impact on subsequent development, or they may be early warning signs of later and more significant problems. Remember, we're looking for *patterns* of atypical behavior, not just sporadic instances. Parents (and teachers) should note the dates and times of occurrence, the duration and frequency of behavior, the type of activity (language, fine motor, etc.), and any difficulty interacting with peers.

There is a world of difference between a skill that is delayed and one that is disordered. Great care should be taken to distinguish between skills that are slow in emerging and those that are different in quality, form, and function.

How we do that is covered in the following chapter.

Chapter 3

"He's Fine—He'll Grow Out of It": Delay vs. Learning Disability

"Oh, no, don't worry," says the teacher or pediatrician or well-meaning friend. "There's nothing wrong—he's just developing more slowly than the others. He'll catch up."

How many mothers have heard some variation of this statement? As I explained earlier, it can be quite difficult to differentiate between a minor delay in development and a learning disability. For those children who would benefit from early intervention, this lack of clarity can cause a parent to lose valuable time.

Remember Helen, the mother who suspected a problem when she heard her son Michael's inability to rhyme? This is how she tells it:

"I went to the preschool and the children were all drawing self-portraits. There was quite a variety of levels because the kids ranged in age from three to five. Even so, my son's self-portrait seemed very immature. I thought, 'Oh well, he's not at their level,' but it was more than that. He couldn't make a complete circle for the face, and there were no eyes. I'm not one of those mothers who panic at the first sign of something, but I couldn't help but notice that there were other things going on. His writing wasn't as clear as the other kids'. He couldn't write his name when the others did, and when he finally could, some of the letters were backward, and sometimes the entire word was written backward. I brought it up to the teachers and they would say, 'Oh, don't worry, it's common'—and it *is* common. It's hard to tell early on whether this is a problem waiting to happen or just how kids do things when they are exploring what we adults know as reading and writing.

"I didn't really see Michael's unusual self-portrait as a sign of a problem, the same way I didn't see his not being able to rhyme as a real problem. They definitely concerned me, but I never imagined they could be signs of something truly serious. I saw it as just being part of his course of development. There were older kids in that class too, so I could always put it down as an age-related issue; but then I would compare him with his younger sister. He didn't know all his letters, and Emma was starting to learn hers. Why did he have trouble when his younger sister did not? I asked the teachers what they thought about it."

"And what did they say?" I asked.

"Oh, don't worry, he's doing fine...."

THE THREE D'S: DIFFERENCE, DELAY, AND DISORDER

Most people (including mothers) have trouble figuring out the difference between normal variations in development and learning disabilities. When and how can we know the difference? To answer this question, I spoke to Dr. Sheldon Horowitz of the National Center for Learning Disabilities. He began by talking about what he called the Three Ds: Difference, Delay, and Disorder.

Difference

"Sometimes you will find a child who learns a little differently than the others," he said. "This child whose learning style is different is...different. That's all. No two people learn in exactly the same way. Some children learn best when they hear information as opposed to seeing it in writing. Some catch on to new skills very quickly, and others need to have things explained more than once. These differences are neither good nor bad; they simply are, and it is precisely these individual differences and preferences that make our lives so interesting."

Delay

"Now let's talk about delay," said Dr. Horowitz. "This can be a little confusing, so bear with me. If I'm a child and you have made your best effort to show me how to do something, but I'm still not getting it, that doesn't necessarily mean that something is 'broken.' It may mean that I need a little more experience in that area before I can get it. I may need to grow up a little bit. I may need a little more practice. I may need to have people talking to me about that subject.

"Take math, for example. Some young children learn how to count because it makes sense to them. Others need practice playing with things and stacking them and counting on their fingers before it kicks in. They may be *delayed* in how they acquire those skills and in their ability to understand without instruction. Even after you've given them experiences to help bolster it, they may still be delayed in getting it. When we see a child who is late in talking or who has slow vocabulary development, that is a *delay in development* in what we expect to see over the normal course of development. These delays in development tend to even out, and do not necessarily mean that you're going to have a disorder. But it's worth careful monitoring. And there is definitely no harm in sharing concerns with teachers and others, and doing everything you can to build your child's skills and confidence in early reading, speaking, and listening.

"As I said earlier, the way we talk about delay can be a little confusing, but it's important that parents understand how the term *delay* is used by different professionals for different purposes. If your child is showing signs of delay in learning and behavior in many areas such as walking, talking, understanding directions, listening, and paying attention, it is clear that he or she has some catching up to do. Problems in any of these areas might be cause for concern, but when multiple areas are affected, we often say that the child has signs of *developmental delay*. Note the difference. We earlier talked about a 'delay in development,' and here we are talking about 'developmental delay.' Same words, used in a different order—and that really does matter. A *delay in development* is just that: a delay in development. But the term *developmental delay* suggests something different, something bigger."

At this point I sighed, wondering why the ways we talk about LD and the terms we use are so complicated. Even though they mean well and are there to be helpful, professionals tend to muddy up the words we use to describe even the simplest forms of LD, probably because this is an ever-evolving field. *Dyslexia* becomes *reading disorder* or *language-based learning disability* or *phonological disorder* or *reading disability* and who knows what else. Some professionals have built their names and reputations on coming up with exotic new terms for things that have already been classified under other exotic names. Other professionals, like Dr. Horowitz, spend countless hours trying their best to simplify things so mothers like us can navigate the thickets of terms and labels and therapies and interventions that promise to make things better!

"So what I think you are saying is that there are basically two different types of delay," I repeated. "There is a delay in development, which can involve one or more specific areas, such as a delay in learning to read or do math. And then there is developmental delay, which is more global."

"Yes," Dr. Horowitz said. "In general, when educators and other helping professionals use the term developmental delay, we are concerned not just about a few specific areas of weakness but about many areas of the child's overall development."

"I see how this could be very confusing for mothers!" I said. "And what about professionals? Do you think some of them are interchanging the two terms and saying developmental delay when they actually mean a delay in development?"

"If they do," he said, "it is unfortunate, confusing, and misleading. Words make a difference!"

"They certainly do," I added. "Mothers should bear in mind that if they hear the pediatrician use the words *developmental delay*, they should not immediately panic. They should ask, 'Do you mean a delay in a specific area? Or is it pervasive?'"

"Good advice," said Dr. Horowitz, "and you just used another important word—*pervasive*—that is sometimes used together with the word *developmental*. The label Pervasive Developmental Disorder (or PDD) describes children who share many characteristics of children with autism. Their learning and behavior are 'atypical,' meaning very different from what is expected during the normal course of development."

"How are we, as mothers without a medical background, supposed to be able to interpret all these different possibilities when a pediatrician says *developmental delay?* We certainly don't want mothers to think their child has autism when, in fact, it's a delay in only one area, such as reading."

"The reality is that pediatricians have no crystal ball and are sometimes at a real disadvantage. They rely on reports by parents and other care providers who don't always agree, and have only very brief contact with a child in a less-than-ideal setting. Sometimes the child is too young and it is too early to tell what is really going on, so they will use the label *developmental delay* as an umbrella term to express concern and to help parents secure early intervention services."

"Why would they do that?" I asked. "Why can't they be more specific?"

"Because it's simply too soon to predict what the future will hold and the progress a child will make over time. So the label is used for the purpose of getting the child the right kinds of help as quickly as possible. And keep this in mind: the term *developmental delay* is not one that follows a child throughout the school years. It is a way to open the door to services like specialized instruction, speech-language therapy, or occupational therapy."

"So if we say 'developmental delay' at that early stage," I said, "it does not necessarily mean the child has LD or autism. It's a way to get that child services before it is truly possible to figure out what, if anything, is wrong." I asked how parents get the diagnosis of developmental delay.

"Parents have a number of options, but all roads lead to your local school district. Parents can start by seeking advice from medical providers, including pediatricians, psychiatrists, or neurologists. They can also seek help from a psychologist, speech-language pathologist, or other related service provider. If the professionals who meet your child suspect there might be a problem, you don't want to wait until the child is in school to get him services. He needs help *now*. But you can't actually say he has a speech or language delay *educationally* because the preschool child has no experience yet. How are you going to classify him? So a medical doctor can go ahead and say 'Here's my medical opinion. Using my criteria, I've decided the child has language delay or motor skill delay.'"

"I see," I said. "So, can a medical expert look at a very young pre-school child and say, 'Based on my medical opinion of this child's development, she seems to have some developmental delay, so let's get her into a program?'"

"Yes. And that kind of program takes place before the education system kicks in."

"How do parents find those programs?"

"After getting the medical opinion, you go to the local school dis-trict and you say, 'I need services for my child.' It could be a program within the school or at another location. It is the school district's responsibility to figure out how to provide 'free and appropriate' serv-ices to the child in the 'least restrictive' setting. This will require a for-mal evaluation by the school. These evaluation services are the same whether your child is school-aged or preschool. Don't be reluctant to asks your school district for more information! You are under no obli-gation to do anything, and nothing will be done without your explic-it written consent. Any and all records and reports are, by law, kept confidential. So if you have concerns, asking for help from the school district is a great place to start."

"Are the doctors still involved at that point?" I asked.

"They can offer their opinion as part of the overall evaluation process, but the final determination is made by a committee made up of teachers, parents, specialists (yes, the doctor is part of this team), and, most important, the parents. The team not only decides whether the child qualifies for special services, but works together to set goals for the child's short-term and long-term progress. Once this is done, the school is responsible for finding a program, either within the dis-trict or elsewhere, where these goals can be addressed."

"When you are looking at the broad category of developmental delay as a way to get services for a child, when does it end?" I asked.

"At what age do you reach a point where you say someone is not delayed?"

"The developmental delay category extends through preschool. During the pre-K year and sometimes into kindergarten, it is often easier to put a specific name to specific areas of delay, such as a delay in speech. If not, the developmental delay classification can be used a bit longer, but never past the early elementary grades."

"Let's talk about the role of the mother in all this," I said. "Would you advise a mother to seek immediate help for a young child who is showing delays in development? Or do you sit back and wait?"

"No," Dr. Horowitz said. "You do not sit back and wait. If you are already asking the question, it means that you have concerns, which could lead you to interact with your child in ways that might make things worse! I remember speaking to a mother who was convinced that her son, a late talker and a little clumsy, was not ready to learn to tie his shoes. A half-hour and a few cookies later, this mom's expectations of her son skyrocketed when he showed her his newly learned skill. Had this mom not come to ask for help, her son would have started school needing help with a skill that was well within his reach."

"What do you say to a mother who doesn't want to sound any alarms but who has a feeling that something is not right with her child?" I asked. "For example, one of our mothers, Helen, has a son who couldn't draw a face. His drawing had no eyes, whereas every other child in the class drew faces of people with eyes. Helen saw this as a red flag, but it was not enough to propel her to seek advice from her son's pediatrician. What would you advise in this instance?"

"I would say that very often, observations, impressions, and intuition come together in a sort of flashpoint or 'aha' moment," he said. "That's when most parents know it is time to take action, regardless of what others might say or think. In your example, the missing eyes in a portrait does not suggest a reliable diagnosis or educational classification. But if he still struggles with this after lots of practice drawing faces with eyes and other features, this mom would be wise to watch for other signs or patterns of difficulty with tasks when he is playing with friends or once he begins school.

"*Pattern* is an important word. She should look for patterns. She should ask herself whether there are times when he can do things successfully and other times when he struggles with the same tasks. She should make note of whether he can do something one day but seems to forget how to do it the next. She should pay careful attention to how well he listens to and follows instructions, the progress he is making in learning early reading skills, and the kinds of activities he seeks out and enjoys. A single instance of the child drawing a face without eyes in and of itself is not a problem, but clearly the parent has an obligation to look for patterns. Armed with this information, Helen can make well-informed decisions about how to be an effective advocate for her son and ensure that he gets the help he needs, regardless of what advice others might give."

Now that we've spoken about "differences" and "delays," what can be said when delays don't go away? Some children show signs of delay that seem to remain after targeted help and careful intervention in school and at home. To get these children even more intensive assistance and set realistic goals, we refer to their learning and behavior as being disordered. We can also refer to it as having a learning disability.

Disorder

"We go from delay into LD when we realize that the child's struggles are not a matter of immaturity or lack of opportunity to learn and practice," Dr. Horowitz explained. "A disorder is a condition that is hard-wired in some way. It is who the person is. It is how they think. It is how they function. When you look at families where fathers, sons, and cousins all struggle with learning to read, spell, or write, we can safely assume that there is a shared genetic tie to dyslexia."

"How early can you tell that it is not a difference or delay, but actually a disorder?" I asked.

"It is very hard to pinpoint LD until a child has had some meaningful time in the classroom," he said. "You cannot tell if a pre-K child has LD. And we're talking specifically about LD here. Until the child enters school, you can only point to behaviors and characteristics that place a child 'at risk' for LD."

Often the area where problems are first detected is reading. Dr. Horowitz and I talked about the importance of building a solid foundation of early literacy skills and about the National Center for Learning Disabilities' program called Get Ready to Read! (GRTR!). This is a simple-to-use twenty-item screening tool that can help parents and early educators ascertain whether a preschool child is developing the skills needed to become a reader once instruction begins in kindergarten.

GRTR! was designed to help parents know where their children are along the path to reading readiness. It includes an assortment of activity cards that describe the types of things parents and teachers can do to prepare children for early reading success. It also includes online games and a series of literacy checklists for school and home as reminders of the types of activities that will contribute to and accelerate a child's readiness to learn to read.

Getting ready to read is not something that happens overnight; it is a process that unfolds over a long period of time. It is also one of the areas of early learning that we know the most about. So parents should pay attention to the building blocks for early literacy and find ways to introduce these ideas and to provide lots of practice during the course of everyday activities. In the following section, Dr. Horowitz discusses GRTR! in more detail.

A WORD ABOUT READING

"GET READY TO READ": AN EARLY LITERACY SCREENING TOOL FOR PARENTS AND EDUCATORS

1. How books *work* is a very important concept for young children to understand before they start learning to read.

"Successful readers know how books work. As simple as it sounds, some children need to be shown how to hold a book so the pages can be turned in the right direction. They need to know that pictures and words do different things, and be shown where the title and author's name can be found. Children who are successful readers have experience with books," says Dr. Horowitz. "When someone picks up a book and says 'let's read,' the child should know what to expect so he can focus his attention on the story, the words, and the fun experience that lies ahead."

2. Children learn that there are things called letters that sit behind the reading process.

"If you point to a single letter and then to a picture of a dog, you know that they are different. One is a picture that conveys lots of meaning, and the other is a symbol that represents a sound. Helping children to grow their vocabulary through naming and describing objects and feelings should be a nonstop priority for parents and others who care for young children. Teaching children how letters work, helping them learn the sounds they represent and how they map onto the words we use, is often much more challenging. The goal is to build confidence and skill in both these areas because both are needed for children to become competent readers."

3. Children need to learn about sounds and how they work in words.

"Some children seem to have a knack for reading. With very little instruction or guidance, they figure out how to match letters and sounds and recognize that by combining strings of letters, they can actually read printed words. But this is the exception rather than the rule. Even before a child begins school and formal teaching of reading begins, parents can set the stage for early literacy success by doing simple activities that teach and practice such things as naming letters and saying the sounds they make, naming things that start or end with those sounds, and playing rhyming games."

We live in a world that is filled with words, and children who are delayed in their vocabulary development and their ability to "break the code" for reading are at risk for struggle in school right from the start. "There are some astounding data about the numbers of words that children are exposed to when they enter school," Dr. Horowitz said. "Studies have shown that children whose parents read to them and take them to libraries benefit greatly from rich language experiences versus children whose parents do not read to them.

"This second group of children is exposed to tens of thousands of words prior to age four. The first group is exposed to *millions* of words. Simply by virtue of having that expansive vocabulary available to them, this first group is way ahead when they start listening and start reading. If you do not have that background or exposure, you may have a little more catching up to do."

The best time to catch up is *before* formal reading instruction begins. By third grade, children are reading to learn rather than learning to read. Children who do not have the background that a richer vocabulary provides do not know basic social studies words or history words or animal words or nature words. If they haven't built a solid foundation for the mechanics of reading, they will have to work a little harder in the beginning.

So, mothers, be advised: even if your child doesn't yet understand the meaning of certain words, read to your child, read *with* your child, talk about anything and everything that will introduce new words and ideas, and then do it again!

"And so, to bring the conversation full circle," I said, "whether or not your child has a learning difference, delay, or disorder, you must be a keen observer and gather information about how your child is developing in all areas. You must talk to the pediatrician about any patterns of behavior you observe (areas of strength as well as areas of concern). And finally, you must sit down in a chair, or climb into bed with your child, and read, read, read."

Fortunately, most mothers do read a lot with their children, but others have so little time due to work and family obligations that they find it all too easy to plop their child down in front of the television instead of taking the time to open a book. It may be that the mother herself has trouble reading. In any case, mothers need to take charge and make sure to carve out a few precious minutes every day to open a book and read with their preschool child. Let your child turn the pages. Point at letters and words as you read the story aloud. Point to the pictures and describe what you see. It sounds simple, but these things really make a difference!

Every minute you spend with your child and a book brings him or her that much closer to success as a reader—and brings you closer to an awareness of patterns that may be an indication of one of those three Ds: difference, delay, or disorder.

Chapter 4
Am I Alone in This?

Your intuition is on high alert. You suspect your child is having trouble learning to read. She can't seem to remember her letters, or has trouble recognizing simple words. Maybe there is a problem with socialization. Nothing is clear yet, nothing you can point to with certainty; and yet you feel that something isn't quite right. You make your first tentative moves to alert others, and what happens? "Oh, no, he's fine," you hear from your mother. "Look at her—there's nothing wrong," your husband tells you. The teachers at your daughter's kindergarten or nursery school tell you not to worry because she will grow out of it. The pediatrician thinks you are overreacting.

Is it any wonder you feel alone? Is it any wonder you begin to think (with even a little bit of hope), "Well, maybe they are right."

But how long does that last?

Those nagging suspicions will *not* go away, no matter how much you try to banish them from your thoughts.

If you find yourself in this situation now, or once did before your child was eventually evaluated and found to have LD, you are in good company. Thousands, maybe millions, of mothers have had to ask themselves this basic question: "Am I alone in this?" Some even go further and ask, "Am I *crazy?* Why am I the only one who can see this?"

Lisa definitely felt that way. "I was home with my son Ryan all day," she said. "My husband would come home after working two jobs and spend fifteen minutes with him and watch him do what kids do and say, 'He looks fine to me!' It was always difficult to look at Ryan and see a problem. No one would have looked at him and said, 'Oh, my God, there's something wrong with that kid.' His nature is such that he tries so hard to be good. A lot of people in school or society don't equate a kid who is good as someone with special needs. They think there should be a behavior problem involved. If your child doesn't have a behavior problem, he doesn't fit that mold and they won't see it.

"Of course, all of this made me question myself and my own judgment. My mother-in-law thought he was perfect. The school thought he was perfect. I would bring my concerns to the preschool teacher but get, 'Oh, he's fine, he's fine.' My husband would say, 'Lisa, if the school says he's fine, he's fine.' You would think I would be reassured by that, but honestly, it only added to my frustration. I *knew* there was something wrong.

"When other kids were forming groups, Ryan would play by himself. I would look at the teachers and ask, 'Is that OK?' They would say 'Oh, yes, he's a great kid, he doesn't have any behavior issues.' My pediatrician said the same thing when I brought up my concerns: 'You're a new mom, you're overprotective, you're overreacting.' I asked for Ryan's records because I wanted to take him to another pediatrician, and when I read them I actually became embarrassed: there it was, written down in black and white. 'Mother called *again*. Mother says she 'knows something is wrong' *again*. Mother overreacting.' And I thought, Wow, they really didn't like me."

Deborah, too, knew there was something wrong when her daughter Windy was very young, and like Lisa, she was the only one who could see it. "I just knew there was something wrong," she said. "Windy was talking early so you couldn't really detect any obvious problems, but there was something about her that I could see and no one else seemed to notice. I don't know how, but I just *knew* something wasn't right. When she was in kindergarten, the teacher said she noticed something, too. She didn't tell me at first because, like me, she didn't know what it was and she didn't want to alarm me without reason. Eventually she came to me and said, 'I don't know what's wrong, but I feel something isn't right.' I went to the pediatrician and he said, 'Oh, no, she's fine. You're just an overreacting mother. This is your first child.'

"That was a real problem at the very beginning. I couldn't get any professional to affirm what I sensed. Windy's high verbal skills helped her along the way, but they also caused other people to say she didn't have any sort of a problem at all. My family didn't understand, either. At first, my husband's reaction was to say, 'Deborah, she's fine.' And my mother was actually angry with me. She never saw anything wrong, and she never accepted the fact that there might be a problem—even later, when it became obvious to everyone. So, essentially, at the beginning I was alone for the journey."

It would be wonderful if every mother in these earliest days of LD could find a supportive friend, especially if that friend is another mother going through the same ordeal. Deborah became that friend for me, but our daughters were both teenagers by the time we met. Most mothers will eventually connect with others, but it's not easy to do at this early stage. Most of the mothers in existing support groups have already undergone some of the rigors of LD. They have already had their child evaluated, and more than likely are dealing with Special Education issues. As a mother now in the earliest stages of your journey with LD, you may not have the courage (or desire!) to meet with mothers of students already established in Special Education. You may be unsure of your suspicions. You may be reluctant to say anything, especially after being shot down so many times before whenever you have dared venture an opinion.

It appears to be a lonely road, but rest assured, there are fellow travelers. You may even know someone who is going through the exact same thing, but like you, is fearful of reaching out and taking that first step. You can try to look to people around you for support—your husband, your child's teachers, your mother, your best friend—but no one will truly empathize as will another mother who is going through the exact same thing.

In a later chapter we will discuss your next steps and how to go about getting your child evaluated, regardless of the opposition you face at home and in the school. But first, there is another type of mother I would like to discuss, the one who is *not* the first to detect a problem.

Chapter 5
"Just Let Him Be Three": Forms of Denial

"I used to read the book *Oh, the Places You'll Go!* to my son," Dana tells me. "It's by Dr. Seuss. There is a picture in that book that really hits home. The character is standing in front of hundreds of different roads, not knowing which one to take. That was exactly how I felt: paralyzed, confused, not knowing which way to go or where to go or even how to start."

Dana's son James has one of the related disorders we cover in this book—generalized anxiety disorder—and his mother's emotional experience is a valuable illustration of how some of us stumble a bit when first confronted by our challenges. I put myself in this category, by the way. I was not one of those mothers who approach the teacher. I had to be told, and then shown, and then forcibly confronted by the problem before I could accept it.

Dana and I both spent significant periods of time in denial, but we had differing forms of denial. Mine was outward. Once I accepted the situation, I took the necessary actions but spent years in isolation, denying to the outside world that anything was wrong. Dana, on the other hand, had a great deal of trouble actually taking action to start dealing with the issue. Her situation could better be described as paralysis than denial.

DANA'S STORY: PARALYZED INTO INACTION

"My son started preschool when he was three and a half," she said, "and I can tell you that when we walked into that preschool we had no concerns at all. There was a little separation anxiety—no, that's a serious understatement. The first few weeks were horrendous; at one point, the teacher had to take this hysterical little boy into the hallway so that the rest of the class could start their day. He was crying so hard that she was afraid he was going to vomit. I ended up seeing this scene by accident, as James had forgotten his backpack and I had run home to get it. I will never, ever get the image of his little face out of my head. It took everything I had not to run in and grab him.

"He had a preschool teacher who was quite wonderful. One of her favorite things about teaching was to conduct individual assessments of children, where they have to identify letters and things like that. She would send us progress reports that said he knew some of his letters, like A, B, and C, but didn't know D, E, and F. We knew darn well that he *did* know his letters and numbers, so it was quite a surprise to receive those comments. Something wasn't matching up. We knew the way he was at home, and the teacher was coming at us with things we knew couldn't be right.

"About halfway through that first year of preschool, we started to get comments that he was distracted. The teacher would mention this casually now and then when I picked him up after school. Eventually, she called to tell me that James had turned his back during storytime. I could pass off all the other things she told me as normal or a minor occurrence, but when he turned his back on the others…there was something not quite right with that.

"The trouble is, there is such a fine line between being simply distracted and indications of a real problem. My eyes were open. I was paying attention. But I wasn't rushing to do any sort of official evaluation. To be honest with you, I was *very* nervous about going into the school system with Special Education and evaluations, so I didn't do anything. It was a simple matter of distraction, as far as I was concerned. It would clear itself up eventually. That's what I thought. That's what I hoped.

"One day my husband called me at the office to tell me that James had lost his recess. They had been playing a parachute game in gym— they have a big piece of cloth that they all lift into their air, and when the parachute is up the kids are supposed to run under it and switch sides before it comes down again. Instead of doing that, my son sat down in the middle of the circle. He was punished for it. They took away his recess. At first, when I heard the story, I laughed and thought, 'Good! He's finally showing his obstinate side, he's finally getting comfortable at school.' But when I thought more about it, it didn't seem right.

"My husband had picked my son up after school that day and asked him about it. James said, 'I was just confused, Dad.' I called the teacher and as we talked, it became clear to both of us that it was not a behavior issue at all. It happened due to an inability to understand the directions. He wasn't doing it to show his obstinacy—I wish he had been!

"Soon after that, the teacher said she thought he might have an auditory processing disorder. That was the first time I ever heard those words. I think she said it that way because she wanted to tell me something more than 'he's just distracted.' At first, I was a little worried, but I was also frustrated that she wasn't getting to see how smart he was. I still had trouble believing there was anything seriously wrong. He wasn't distracted at home. He was a smart, happy little boy at home, and didn't seem to have any issues at all. It frustrated me and made me sad that the teacher couldn't see this side of him. In some ways it was denial on my part. He seemed fine at home, therefore I simply couldn't accept the possibility that he might not be fine at school.

"But I started researching. I found everything I could on auditory processing disorders. I took every tidbit the teacher told me and researched it and pored over it to figure out for myself whether or not she was correct.

"Feelings of panic began to creep up within me. Every time the teacher said something about distraction, I would smile and nod, but inside I was twisted in knots. I would come home and I would be worried, I would be panicky, and I would try to have a conversation with my husband about it; but every conversation turned into, 'You're blowing this out of proportion, they don't know what they're talking about, we know him so much better.'

"It was very hard to go forward without support from my partner. Had he been as concerned as I was, we probably would have taken action sooner. But with something that seemed so vague, it was hard to know when to take action and *how* to take action, and how to do it by myself.

"My boss happens to be a very good friend, and she has a son who has dyslexia. They didn't figure it out until ninth grade. At one point in high school he tried to take an honors class and was told he couldn't take it because his records said he had LD. This was back in the eighties, and I don't think things are the same now, but that experience influenced my boss's opinion about my situation. She had good intentions, but when I talked to her about getting my son evaluated, she would say, 'Don't do it, don't do it, he'll be labeled for life!' I was terrified. Had I not already had my own fears about labels and the whole sense of being overwhelmed, maybe I would have acted sooner. But I didn't.

"I had no other support system at that time. I had no one to talk to. The ones who were closest to me were advising me to go against what my gut told me I had to do. I was paralyzed, and I still feel guilt about that. I wonder if I had moved sooner, would it have been better? Would I have saved him some days that were harder on him than they should have been? Had I known what to do, had I fully accepted what the teachers were telling me, had I been able to absorb the information and straighten it out in my head, would everything have been better for him? Of course it would, and that's what I feel guilty about.

"Now I know that I should have acted the minute I heard the words *auditory processing disorder*. I should have taken him to a pediatrician that day, but I didn't. Why not? Why was there so much resistance on my part? I ask myself that question every day, and this is what I come up with: it is very hard when you are rearing a child with a partner, and that partner is saying there is nothing wrong. Basically he is saying that you are being paranoid and ridiculous. Meeting that resistance from your partner, day after day—I can't stress enough what a huge obstacle that can be.

"It was a sickening feeling at the time. It put real stress on the marriage. You feel like you're doing things on the sly. The day I came home and told my husband I was going to have our son evaluated, I had to prepare myself for his reaction. 'I think you're making the wrong decision,' he said. 'I think you're making it a bigger deal than it needs to be, and I think that you are going to give him a sense that something is wrong with him when nothing is wrong at all.' Those words reinforced all my biggest fears. And, of course, he had some valid points! So it would freeze me all over again. I would make a decision to go forward, and then we would talk or argue about it, and the thought of 'What if he's right?' would paralyze me.

"While that was going on at home, I had the teacher at school pushing me to get James evaluated. Every time she said it, I brushed her off. 'Just let him be three,' I pleaded, and then, 'Let him be four,' almost as if the evaluation would somehow *create* the problem rather than officially acknowledge a problem that was already there. She didn't agree with my decision, but she didn't argue with me. She said, 'We can continue to watch the situation. It's up to you entirely, but I think he would benefit from an evaluation.'

"I couldn't do anything. I couldn't make up my mind. I didn't know where to turn, and might still be in that state of mind had I not had a friend who had already gone through something similar. She stood in my driveway with me one day, and literally took me by the shoulders and shook me. 'Dana, you have *got* to do this!' she said. That's what it took to finally break down and face the truth.

"I finally got up the courage to go to the school and give my consent. I remember bursting into tears immediately afterward, and the teacher looked a little shocked. 'Dana, he is going to be fine!' She was so reassuring, and I *so* needed to hear that. So I gave my consent in February to have him evaluated. He was found to have generalized anxiety disorder, and he's now receiving the services he needs.

"If I met a mother who was going through what I went through, the first and the most important thing I would do is to acknowledge her feelings and say that, yes, the situation *is* overwhelming, and that yes, of course, you *are* going to stand there like a deer in the headlights because you don't know where to start. You don't even know what the problem *is*, so how do you know where to start? And so you are literally standing there, frozen, like the character in *Oh, the Places You'll Go!*, staring out at all those different roads. You just don't know where to go, which road to take. You don't know who to listen to. I had two very important people in my life, my husband and my boss, telling me to leave it alone; and I had professionals telling me *not* to leave it alone; and then I also had something in my gut telling me to latch onto this and try to figure out what it is.

"I look back now and realize I was overwhelmed by it all. I look back at these gaps when I did nothing at all—and I *knew* they were gaps even when I was in them. I felt awful that these gaps were happening, when no action was being taken because I wasn't sure what to do. It's so awful, not knowing what to do, because you're *supposed* to know what to do. You're the mom. But when you don't know what to do, you feel like such a terrible mother.

"So that is my advice: if you can align yourself with somebody who has been through the system, that is what will save you. My friend in the driveway also handed me a stack of books, books that were full of information. By doing that she was also saying, 'I have these books because I have been through this already.' Our take on things might be different, and our approaches are different, and our situations are different, but the fact is that we have some things that are exactly the same. Our feelings, our fears, our frustrations and worries were very similar.

"Sometimes when we would meet at the bus stop in the morning, all I had to do was roll my eyes and sigh, and she knew *exactly* what I was talking about. That was huge, to know I had somebody else out there who understood."

MY STORY: IGNORING THE EVIDENCE

Of all the mothers I interviewed, none were in as much denial as I was regarding my child's disability. Mine was not total denial: it was a strange, partial form of denial, as if I somehow acquired the ability to rope off whole sections of my life while continuing to carry on with all the others as normally as possible. Soon after learning Allegra had a disability, I compartmentalized it. I found help for her, and schools for her, and yet I never really accepted the situation.

Unlike most mothers, my intuition didn't kick in as it should have. Certainly, I saw things, but I never connected them to anything serious, and I had to be told point-blank that there was a problem.

On Allegra's first day of nursery school, we walked hand in hand down the street, singing songs and pretending we were not a little apprehensive. She was to attend the Madison Avenue Presbyterian Day School in New York City, which was on the ninth floor of a building above the church. The school entrance was jammed with mothers and fathers anxious to meet the teachers.

She loved school and loved her classmates, and there was not a single sign of trouble on the horizon. Few mothers thirty years ago would be looking for early warning signs of LD or any other disorder when their child entered nursery school, even if there was an obvious problem. Most of us would put it down to a million other things: she's tired, she's just not paying attention, she's got some behavior issues, it's nothing serious, there's nothing really *wrong*.

And indeed, I cannot think of a single thing that went wrong that first year. Allegra's teachers never indicated there might be a problem. She was energetic, maybe a little hyperactive, but nothing out of the ordinary. And so it went for the first year. When she returned to the same nursery school for a second year, all was well again...for the first couple of months. And then the phone rang.

Miss Zimmerman, the headmistress, asked if she could schedule an appointment to meet with me. I readily agreed, and didn't even bother to ask the reason. I assumed it was a meeting offered to all parents to discuss their child's progress and plans for kindergarten the following year.

I went to the school, calm and optimistic, even a little excited at the idea of discussing Allegra's bright future as a kindergartner. Miss Zimmerman led me into her office and closed the door. I remember suddenly hearing a small voice inside whispering, "Uh-oh...something's wrong."

She began by praising Allegra, though after each sentence of praise she added a qualifying "but."

"But she doesn't follow directions."

"But she can't seem to pay attention."

"But she seems to retreat into a world of her own."

"But she can't keep up with the others."

Miss Zimmerman tried as hard as possible to cushion these statements. She was a naturally kind woman, and knew it could not be easy for any mother to hear such things about her child. She ended by suggesting I have Allegra tested.

I immediately panicked, thinking there was something wrong with her, a virus or condition neither I nor the pediatricians could see. I tried as hard as I could to remain calm as I asked, "Tested for what?"

Miss Zimmerman leaned forward and said I should have her tested for learning problems.

I sat back, relieved that it wasn't anything truly serious. It was just a small matter, a "learning problem," something easily remedied. My relief was quickly followed by confusion. *Learning problems...*what exactly does that mean? Does she have learning problems because she can't follow directions? But that's Allegra! She's like that at home, too. It's not a learning problem.

Miss Zimmerman pressed on and told me she thought Allegra might have difficulty in a regular kindergarten. I assured her, "No, my daughter won't have a problem. I'm sure of it. She gets along with everyone. She loves her teachers. She learns everything."

Miss Zimmerman undoubtedly had much experience with mothers who refused to believe their child had a problem. She smiled and said, "This isn't easy to hear, I know," and again, she repeated, "but I really do believe she'll have trouble in a regular kindergarten."

This time the word *regular* stuck out. I wondered what it could mean. If a kindergarten wasn't regular, what else could it possibly be? Had she used the words *learning disabilities,* I'm not sure I would have understood what they meant, either. "Is all this because she won't sit still?" I asked, amazed. Surely this was a minor problem, irritating for the teachers perhaps, and a bit embarrassing for me, but surely it wasn't a sign of something serious.

This was not how things were supposed to be. I was supposed to enroll Allegra in one of the local kindergartens, I hoped the one my son had attended. She would go there with my friend's children who were the same age, and with many of her new friends from nursery school. That was the reality I had set out for her, and I wasn't about to change it, especially over what I believed was a behavior problem.

I vowed to start working with her that night. We would sit down and go through things over and over until she could work through these problems. I knew she could do it. I said that to Miss Zimmerman, and she suggested I come to Parents Day so I could see the situation with my own eyes.

I reminded her that I had been to Parents Day already. I had been to several Parents Days and never once had I seen a problem.

"That was last year," she said. "Things have changed."

Miss Zimmerman's words stayed with me until I got home, but by then, I had already decided that she was wrong. She didn't know Allegra as well as I did. I understood my daughter's behavior. I knew what she could and couldn't do. We would work together to overcome these problems, whatever they were.

Denial had entered my life for the first time.

I went to Parents Day, determined to explain away Allegra's behavior as normal and "that's just who she is." But there it was, staring me in the face, all the things Miss Zimmerman said. But did I see it for what it was? No. I saw *something*, but not the reality of the situation.

The children sat in a tight semicircle on the floor in front of the teacher, listening in rapt attention to a story she was reading. But one child wasn't there. She was off in a corner by herself, pretending to cook lunch for the class, seemingly oblivious to the story, the teacher, and the other children. As Miss Zimmerman said, she had retreated into her own world.

I wanted more than anything to go to her, to take her by the hand and lead her back to the others and say, "No, honey, sit here," but, instead, I forced myself to sit there and watch. Other mothers turned to me once in a while with an awkward smile.

Playtime followed the reading circle, and once again Allegra moved off into another area of the room, where she played a solitary game with her imagination as her only companion. On the few occasions when she did venture toward the other children, they seemed to move away—not because they didn't like her but because they didn't understand her. She seemed a little unreal to them, as if they somehow sensed her preference for her imaginary world over the world they saw around them.

I was embarrassed by all of this. No wonder Miss Zimmerman said the things she did. There was nothing wrong with Allegra (as far as I was concerned), so why was she acting this way?

I then recalled other things, small things that seemed unimportant at the time, but that stayed with me all the same. She couldn't sit still at bedtime when I read to her. Alessandro never had trouble when he was young. He would lie beside me, taken in by the story and my voice. Allegra could never do that. She fidgeted and fussed, and no matter what I did, I couldn't seem to get her attention. Once again it was, "Oh, well, that's just who she is."

Such earlier experiences lay before me in plain sight, but I wasn't connecting the dots. I saw them as isolated incidents, not as a whole, and certainly not cause for concern or panic.

I so wish that I had been able to accept Miss Zimmerman's recommendations without a fight. I wish I had been able to look past my own, unrealistic perceptions of my daughter; I could never quite abandon my vision of her future with all its perfection. I could not come to terms with the idea that something might be wrong, even when I saw the evidence with my own eyes.

Accepting reality can be extremely difficult for parents, but trust me: denial and delay do nothing to alleviate the problems. They only push things down the road a bit, and often make them infinitely worse than they might have been had they been faced squarely and realistically when first encountered. When, and if, someone tells you there might be a problem with your child, do not dismiss it out of hand. Don't panic, either. Listen and observe. Really *look* at your child. Chances are good that you, like me, will suddenly connect the dots and realize that, yes, the teachers are concerned for a reason.

Some of us push away the truth, even when it's staring us in the face. But you cannot avoid reality for long. Trouble comes regardless, mostly because denial does absolutely nothing to change the situation. We can be in denial that the sun is going to come up tomorrow morning. Does the sun care? No. There it is, rising above the horizon.

It is the same with learning disabilities. Does LD care that you don't believe in it? No. There it is, in front of your eyes, whether or not you choose to see it. And once you do see it, don't shrink from it and don't let your fear of "labeling" prevent you from taking action.

A WORD ABOUT LABELS

"I don't want her to be labeled." That is the number-one thing I hear from mothers who are reluctant to have their child tested or receive services, and it concerns me. We can choose to disapprove of those mothers who recoil from the label *special* or *learning-disabled*, but the better path would be to understand their fears, some of which are grounded in the realities of life today.

I know a mother who used to get up at 4:30 every morning to drive her child to a tutor. She went in the dark of early morning so no one would see them—all this to prevent the label *Special Education* from sticking to her son.

I will never forget talking to a mother who had sent her child to a parochial school. The laws regarding separation of church and state required the federally funded Special Education programs to take place in a trailer parked at the edge of the school playground. Her young son had no chance to slip down a hallway into a classroom that looked exactly like all the others. He had to cross the playground in full view of his classmates in the schoolyard or watching from the window, and go to the dreaded "trailer." Think about what it was like for him: walking that endless walk across the playground, books clutched close to his chest, head bowed, eyes cast downward, burning at the thought of his friends watching him from afar. Children who are not in Special Education services are not renowned for their tolerance and acceptance of children who are.

That is what lies behind a mother's distress at the idea of labeling. She, too, was once a student, and quite possibly remembers her own feelings about classmates in Special Ed.

But what is the alternative? The need for Special Education will remain whether we call it *special* or any other term we might come up with to minimize the impact.

Another term that gets us into trouble is *normal*. It sounds harmless enough until we realize that its antonym is *abnormal*—we don't mind hearing our children spoken of as "normal" but I, for one, would slip into mother-tigress mode if I ever heard someone call one of my children "abnormal."

In talking to a group of parents of autistic children, I noticed they were using the words *atypical* and *typical* to describe their children with and without a disability.

I have no problem with that, do you? *Atypical*. Lots of interesting and dynamic people can be thought of as atypical. It has the sound of someone marching to the beat of his own drum, of someone unconventional who does not follow the crowd.

One of our Special Mothers, Janie, brought up the subject of labeling when talking about her husband's reaction to her son's diagnosis with learning disabilities. "He was really concerned about the label," Janie said. "He would say to me, 'What are people going to say?' Eventually I said to him, 'It doesn't matter what people say because they'll be saying a lot worse things if we don't get him some help and he isn't able to finish school.'"

It all comes down to that.

If our children need services, we simply cannot be put off by labels that we find objectionable. Some parents prefer the term *learning differences* to *learning disabilities*.

It's important to emphasize, however, that a child with a "difference" will not qualify for special services; only a child with a diagnosed disorder/disability may qualify.

Learning disabilities are not a disease like chicken pox or mumps. Your child can't catch them from a classmate. There is no cure. They are lifelong, but their effects can certainly be lessened with proper intervention. Hiding your head in the sand will help absolutely no one—not you, not your family, and most definitely not your child.

So let's make peace with the word *special*. It's with us, whether we like it or not. Acknowledge your fears and objections, and look at the word again as it was meant to be, as an adjective used to define someone who truly *is* special in our eyes.

Chapter 6
What Should You Do First?

Some mothers (like me) have or once had trouble facing the reality of their child's problem. Others have no such trouble and go too far in the opposite direction, panicking at the first sign of something they see as atypical. We need to try to come down somewhere between these two extremes.

The way to do this is to truly accept the role that will be yours for many years to come: Your Child's Best Advocate.

"Well, of course," you say. "I have *always* been an advocate for my child" and, of course, you are correct in saying that. But advocacy for a child with learning disabilities entails a lot more stamina and courage than the advocacy we naturally extend to all our children.

In the coming chapters, I will guide you step by step on how to become the very best advocate possible, but right now, in these earliest stages, I would like you to accept and get used to the word *advocate* and apply it to yourself. You are no longer just a mother, wife, sister, daughter, friend, worker. You must now add the word *advocate* to your list of honors.

It will not be easy, and there will be days, weeks, and even months when you want to throw in the towel, though the chances are good that you'll never throw it in completely. The chances are also good that you know all of this already. Even for those of us who have a difficult time accepting reality, our Mother's Intuition has already spoken and said, "I have to do this. No one else will. No one else loves my child as deeply as I do. No one else knows my child as well as I do. No one else is as interested in making sure my child is set on a course for the brightest, happiest future possible."

Listen to that voice. Let it guide you to seek the help you need. Don't try to go through this alone. Find someone, anyone, who will accept and understand what you are going through. Hundreds of thousands of mothers are in the same boat with you. Some of them have already fought many of the battles you now face and can give you invaluable advice on how to proceed. Others are just starting out, too, and, like you, need a shoulder to cry on and someone to listen. Help one another. There are great friendships in your future, if you allow them to flourish.

Now let's talk specifics. I can best do this by answering some of the questions pertaining to early childhood that come up during my speaking engagements.

Q: *My child is a preschooler. How can someone become an advocate for a child who hasn't entered school yet? Am I moving too fast? Should I wait until he is in school?*

A: Being an advocate means knowing how to ensure that your child gets the help he or she needs to be successful. For children who experience learning difficulties, it's never too early to start looking for ways to help them succeed in learning. Even before formal schooling starts, there are things you can do to make sure your child gets help early, so that learning can be a fun and productive experience.

A federal law called the *Individuals with Disabilities Education Act (IDEA) guarantees* certain rights to preschool children through your state's Child Find program (explained on page 51).

The National Center for Learning Disabilities outlines the following first steps you should take if you suspect that your child has difficulty learning:

- *Observe Your Child* and start a record of the behavior you think suggests learning delays or difficulties. (I cover the topic of keeping records in more detail in chapter 9.)

- *Talk to Your Child About What You Are Observing.* Try to learn more about the problems he or she appears to be having through playing with your child, and by observing your child at play with other children, so that you can share specific examples with people who might be able to help. Be sure to enthusiastically praise your child's successes and good efforts often.

- *Meet With Your Child's Pediatrician*, bringing along your list of observations. Be open and honest about your concerns and don't be afraid to ask questions like "Why is my child having trouble?" or "Is this something that will go away by itself?" or "Is this within the normal range of development?" Ask if developmental screenings are available, or whether another medical professional (i.e., a neurologist) or an early childhood specialist (i.e., speech/language pathologist, psychologist, special educator) should evaluate your child. If you are concerned about your child's progress, don't wait to pursue further evaluation.

- *If You Get No Satisfaction, Don't Be Afraid to Go to Another Pediatrician.* This is for the mother who hears, "Oh, he's fine, you're just overreacting." And please resist the temptation to breathe a sigh of relief and think: "I guess I was wrong all along." Trust *your* judgment!

- *Ask the Pediatrician or Your Local School District to Make a Referral* to Child Find, or to the referring agency you should contact to arrange an evaluation for your child. An evaluation will provide you with the information you need to make important decisions, and will determine whether your child could be eligible for early intervention or preschool services. Evaluation findings are strictly confidential. It is up to you to decide with whom the information is shared.

Early Intervention Services are services *for infants and toddlers up to age two* that are designed to identify and address a problem or delay as early as possible.

Preschool Services are specially designed programs offered by public schools and are available for eligible children with disabilities beginning at age three.

Once you request an evaluation, it is your right to have it completed within a set period of time, usually within sixty school days of your signing a written consent for your child to be evaluated. Don't be shy about calling or visiting the evaluation site to keep the process moving.

Bring all information about your child that you think is relevant to meetings and evaluations. When speaking to doctors, therapists, or school administrators, be prepared to tell them your observations about your child.

What Is Child Find?

Child Find is a component of the *Individuals with Disabilities Education Act (IDEA)* that requires states to identify, locate, and evaluate all children with disabilities, aged birth to twenty-one, who are in need of early intervention or Special Education services. Child Find requires all school districts to identify, locate, and evaluate *all* children with disabilities, regardless of the severity of their disabilities.

It is part of IDEA's *Early Intervention Program for Infants and Toddlers with Disabilities*, established in 1986 in recognition of "an urgent and substantial need" to:

- enhance the development of infants and toddlers with disabilities
- reduce educational costs by minimizing the need for Special Education through early intervention
- minimize the likelihood of institutionalization and maximize independent living
- enhance the capacity of families to meet their child's needs

States participating in the program must ensure that early intervention will be available to every eligible child and his or her family. The program is administered through a state agency. (These can vary from state to state. For example, in Delaware it is administered through that state's Department of Health and Social Services, and in Maine, through the State Department of Education.)

You can find the contact information for your state on the web at www.nectac.org/contact/ptccoord.asp. For those without access to a computer, I suggest you start by calling your state Department of Education. Someone there will be able to guide you to the right place.

These are your tax dollars at work—make use of them!

Q: *I think my child needs an evaluation. Where do I go? Who do I talk to? What do I do now?*

A: This question leads us right straight into part II of the book, which will help guide you through the maze of evaluations.

Before we move on, I want to emphasize once more your new role as advocate in your child's life. There will be challenges ahead, and even now, in these first days when you only suspect something may be wrong or you've just heard a teacher tell you that she suspects something is wrong, you can be forgiven for believing that the future has suddenly become a little more daunting and uncertain than before. This is a whole new world for you. Reports will come your way that you will find next to impossible to decipher. Doctors may give you conflicting advice and diagnoses. You may find yourself in conflict with your child's school, and may even come to believe they are "out to get" you. You will experience a range of unwelcome emotions about your own child, such as embarrassment, anger, and disappointment, while at the same time, or quickly after, you will be overwhelmed with pride and love. You will find old friendships strained and find new friendships you never imagined only a few weeks before. You will sometimes feel unappreciated in your efforts, but trust me, that doesn't matter in the end. No one but other mothers in your situation can truly appreciate the hard work and mental and emotional anguish we face. Those mothers will invariably be part of your new network of friends. And if you aren't given a medal at the end of it all, so what? *You* will know that you have stepped up and done your best for your child, and that becomes your true reward.

PART II

The Diagnosis

Chapter 7

One Last Step Before the Diagnosis: Pre-Referral Services

Supreme Court Justice Sonia Sotomayor gave her opinion on a case involving a professor with a law degree who has dyslexia and who sued the New York State Board of Law Examiners for the right to accommodations when taking the bar exam. According to an article in the *New York Times*, Judge Sotomayor remarked that "the field of learning disabilities is replete with chaos, with little agreement among experts on what constituted a disability or how to measure it." She then gave a fine explanation for the reason why so many professionals prefer the word *evaluation* over *diagnosis* when talking about LD. "A learning disability," she said, "is not measurable in the same way a blood disease can be measured in a serum test."

She had it exactly right: LD is a *disorder*, not a disease. James Wendorf, executive director of the National Center for Learning Disabilities, says, "The word *diagnosis* is used less and less often because it has such a clinical sound to it. We more often use *evaluation*, which is a process that a child goes through in order to determine cognitive functioning and identify whether or not there is a learning disability or a related disorder such as ADHD. The word *evaluation* also refers to a product—you get an evaluation, which is the formal report on the various kinds of assessments that have been conducted to identify whether or not there is an issue, and if so, what is the particular type of issue and what the problem might be."

No matter which word we use, for mothers, that word is simply a shorthand way to say what we really mean, which is this: *Something is wrong, and I want to find out what it is.*

In part I, we covered many of the fears that arise before the evaluation. In part II, we shall cover those that occur during the evaluation process, along with an explanation of the process itself. Much of the material is based on the *Parent Guide to the Individuals with Disabilities Education Act (IDEA)* from the National Center for Learning Disabilities. NCLD created this guide to help you become an informed and effective partner with the school in supporting your child's special learning and behavioral needs. Together, this book and the *IDEA Parent Guide* will guide you through the process, from pre-referral services through formal evaluations and beyond. You can find the *Guide* on the NCLD Web site at www.ld.org/a-special-mother.

PRE-REFERRAL SERVICES

Some parents and some school districts do not make the leap from suspecting a child has a learning problem to requesting a formal evaluation. If they're not certain, they take an intermediate step called pre-referral services, which is usually set in motion for a student who has not been able to keep up with the class or whose behavior interferes with learning. Pre-referral services are designed to support these students. Your child's teacher may have discussed this kind of support with you. If not, and if you suspect or already know that your child is struggling in school, you should ask to meet with the teacher to discuss your concerns. In response to those concerns (or those expressed by a teacher), the school will likely offer pre-referral interventions as a first step toward improving your child's performance. These interventions are not Special Education services.

To help find the right approach to teaching your child, often called an *instructional method* or *intervention*, the teacher may consult with other teachers, the reading specialist/teacher, the Special Education teacher, counselors, psychologists, and/or other education professionals. Together they will determine the most appropriate services for your child. This determination may involve *informal* educational and behavioral evaluations. If so, do not make the mistake of thinking "my child has already been tested for LD." The *formal* evaluation comes later and is more substantial.

Always ask about the types of teaching methods or interventions the teacher is recommending, so you can understand how your child will be taught and what kind of progress is expected. You always have the right to request a formal evaluation if you don't believe your child is making adequate progress through pre-referral approaches.

The form of pre-referral service a parent is most likely to encounter is called RTI, or Response-to-Intervention.

RESPONSE-TO-INTERVENTION

This education model promotes early identification of students who may be at risk for learning difficulties. It is a process that emphasizes how well students respond to changes in instruction, and often involves tiers of increasingly intense levels of service for students. According to the National Research Center on Learning Disabilities (NRCLD), the essential components of RTI include:

- Monitoring a student's progress in the general curriculum through appropriate screenings or tests (assessments)
- Choosing and implementing a scientifically proven intervention to deal with a student's learning problems
- Following formal guidelines to decide which students are not making sufficient progress or responding to the intervention
- Monitoring how the student responds to the intervention by using assessments at least once a week or once every two weeks
- Making sure the intervention is provided accurately and consistently
- Determining the level of support that a student needs in order to be successful
- Giving parents notice of a referral and a request to conduct a formal evaluation if a disability is suspected, as required by IDEA

The RTI process has the potential to limit a student's academic challenges and to increase the accuracy of Special Education evaluations. It is also designed to reduce the number of children who are mistakenly identified as having LD when their learning problems are actually due to cultural differences or a lack of adequate instruction. The information gathered by RTI can lead to earlier identification of children who have true disabilities and are in need of Special Education services.

If you don't know whether your child's school has implemented the RTI process or another pre-referral service, now is the time to open up the lines of communication with your child's teacher or school administrators. In order to become an active partner with the school, you must first become an informed parent. You should ask for, and expect to receive, information about your child's needs, the interventions that are being used, who is delivering the instruction, and the academic progress expected for your child. Both the National Center for Learning Disabilities and the National Joint Committee on Learning Disabilities advise parents to ask the following questions:

1. Does our school use an RTI process? (Be aware that your child's school may call the process by another name, such as "problem-solving process" or "multi-tiered system of support." They may have come up with their own name for the procedures, rather than using the specific RTI terminology. Ask if those terms or names are another way of saying RTI.)

2. Are there written materials for parents that explain the RTI process? How can I become involved in the various phases of the RTI process?

3. What interventions are being used and are these scientifically based, as supported by research? (Don't avoid asking the question for fear you may not understand the answer. If you don't understand the answer, ask for an explanation that you can understand. At this stage you are *not* the expert, so don't feel you need to be.)

4. What length of time is recommended for an intervention before determining if my child is making progress?

5. How do school personnel check to be sure that the interventions are being carried out as planned?

6. What techniques are being used to monitor my child's progress and the effectiveness of the interventions? Will the school provide me with regular progress monitoring reports?

7. At what point in the RTI process will I be informed of my due process rights under IDEA, including the right to request an evaluation for Special Education eligibility?

8. When is informed parental consent (your written permission) obtained and when do the Special Education evaluation timelines officially begin under the district's RTI plan?

Staying in frequent communication with the school, receiving information on regular progress (or lack of progress), and participating in decision making should provide you with the information you need to determine whether or not your child should be referred for a formal Special Education evaluation.

Another great resource concerning Response-to-Intervention has been provided to parents by the National Research Center on Learning Disabilities (www.nrcld.org). You can find a free downloadable parent guide called *The ABCs of RTI* at http://nrcld.org/free/downloads/ABC_of_RTI.pdf.

Chapter 8
"Should I Have Him Tested?": Requesting a Formal Evaluation

Many mothers will not go the pre-referral services route but go straight to the formal evaluation. There are several reasons for this: they may not realize the child is having trouble until they are approached by a teacher who advises an evaluation, or they may be so convinced that the child has LD that they feel any further delay would be detrimental.

An evaluation should be a simple procedure. You would think that, wouldn't you? You have finally accepted that there may be a problem with your child, or maybe you have finally convinced others of the potential problem; so the next step should be to go to the school, request an evaluation, study the results, and set your child on course for the specialized instruction, accommodations, and assistance that will bring about educational success. That's the way things should be, and in many cases that is exactly what happens. For other mothers, however, a new challenge appears: how to get the test in the first place, and then how to decipher the results. It is no exaggeration to say that some mothers might as well be handed a sheet of Egyptian hieroglyphics.

One such mother was Helen, whom we met in the first chapter talking about her son Michael in the backseat of the car, unable to rhyme. When I spoke with her about the evaluation process, she said, "I am an attorney. I have a legal background and I researched the laws, and I *still* faced obstacles all along the way when it came to getting the services we needed. I can only imagine how difficult it must be for a mother without legal training when facing the same obstructions and evasions I had to face. Some school systems rely on our ignorance. They count on it."

I asked her to elaborate, and she told me that she believed it all came down to funding: "I know it's not the case in every school, but in my particular situation, I am sure the school was not as forthcoming as they could have been because they had a limited amount to spend on Special Education."

Helen's case is not unusual, but it is important to stress that most schools do not set up roadblocks and hurdles. Indeed, many are proactive in their efforts to provide services, but it would be wishful thinking to believe that every school is forthcoming and helpful. The sad fact remains that some schools face such funding problems that they do not actively seek students eligible for either evaluations or Special Education services. (Here I would like to point out that it is not only a sad fact, but also a direct violation of IDEA. Finding, evaluating, and serving students with disabilities are *not* contingent upon funding levels.)

When Helen's son Michael left preschool and went to kindergarten, they gave him the DIBELS Reading Assessment, designed to quickly identify students at risk for reading failure. "I had no idea they did this test," Helen told me. "I had never even heard of it before. The DIBELS Test showed that my son did not reach the benchmark set for his age group. I wasn't surprised when I heard this—I already suspected that something might be wrong, but I hoped it was just a delay in development and that he was going to catch up with the others. He was way ahead in some things, and I thought he should have been ahead with reading, too, but he wasn't."

"How did you know that?" I asked.

"I volunteered in the classroom once a week," Helen said. "I wanted to see what was being taught, and how far along Michael was in relation to the other kids in the classroom. When the teacher said he wasn't where he was supposed to be, it wasn't a big surprise. I was in the class and I could see for myself.

"They began to pull him out of class to go to a reading specialist [pre-referral services]. I asked the teacher if this indicated a serious problem, but she kept telling me, 'Oh, no, he just needs a little extra help.' So again, I thought—and *hoped!*—that it was all a minor issue with development. Then he went to first grade. I went to the first conference, and they said, 'He's not up to where he should be.' I was a little frustrated because I had been saying that all along. Even so, I put my trust in the idea that the teachers were telling me what was best for him."

"Were they?"

"Well, no," Helen said. "That summer between kindergarten and first grade, I could have sent him to summer school. The earlier you catch this, the better, so, no—they were not telling me what was best for him. The interesting thing is that the teacher *wanted* to tell me, but she couldn't. She was not allowed to come right out and tell me I should have him tested because the school has a limited amount of funding. The trouble is, I didn't know I was supposed to ask. I'm sure I would never have thought to ask the teacher about testing at all—in fact, I *didn't* ask her, not directly. I knew she had a child the same age as Michael, so after she told me that Michael wasn't where he should be in his reading, I said to her, 'If he was your child, would you be doing more for him?' She nodded and I asked, 'What should I do?'

"That's what did it. Those were the magic words, the question that opened the doors. She pulled out a pad and pen and handed them to me, and right there in her office, the teacher dictated the letter I needed to write to her, word for word. That letter requested that my son be evaluated. Now remember, the school had already known for a year that he should be evaluated, but they didn't—or couldn't—take any action until I asked.

"It's a terrible situation. The teachers *wanted* me to ask. They wanted to help. It all comes down to money. It is all budget-related. The order for her to stay silent had to come from her superiors. Her hands were tied. She couldn't do a thing until I wrote a letter asking for the evaluation, but I didn't know a thing about Special Education. I knew nothing about evaluations. I didn't know who to write to, what I was supposed to write. If she hadn't dictated that letter, I don't know what I would have done. At that point I knew I needed to know more, but I had no idea how to move forward. I didn't know the questions, much less the answers. If left on my own, I probably would have had him evaluated eventually, but not through the school. I would have paid for an independent evaluation because I didn't know the evaluation was available through the school.

"I wrote the letter as dictated by the reading specialist and sent it to the school. They contacted me and I filled out the forms giving my consent, and then they conducted the tests."

Helen's situation was extreme, and (I hope!) not common. It certainly does not represent what is *supposed* to be happening. As I mentioned earlier, and once again emphasize here: *schools have an obligation to find, evaluate, and serve students with disabilities, and those obligations are not dependent upon funding levels.*

That is the law. That is what is supposed to happen. In Helen's case, and undoubtedly in many others, it did not.

So here's Lesson #1: if you do not hear a teacher recommend a formal evaluation for your child, do not assume that your child does not need one. Do not assume that no news is good news. If you feel in your gut that something is wrong and that your child is falling behind, you have every right to have your child evaluated by the school at no cost to you. Not all teachers are well trained to spot early learning problems, so parents should not rely exclusively on a teacher's recommendation to evaluate their child. In good schools, a team of people come together to discuss a case and determine the right direction, such as interventions, formal evaluation, or whatever is appropriate.

This goes for children in private or parochial schools as well. If you have a child in a private school, you can still approach the public school and request an evaluation. By law, public schools are required to provide an evaluation for *all* children, not only those directly enrolled in that particular school.

In all cases, the key to moving forward is to submit a *formal written request*. Without that, nothing can be done.

Please note that making a request for a formal evaluation does *not* give the school district your permission to begin Special Education services. It gives permission only to conduct the evaluation. If the evaluation then indicates that your child needs Special Education, the school, in consultation with you, will develop an educational plan tailored to your child's specific needs. At that point, you must again provide written consent for any Special Education services to begin.

You can request a Special Education evaluation at any time, but it's wise to take some preparatory steps first.

1. **Talk to the teacher.** Sounds like a no-brainer, right? But *have* you actually discussed your concerns with the teacher? If not, consider this the first step.

2. **Learn about Special Education services.** Talk to your school's principal about the Special Education services available at your child's school. Inquire about the training and qualifications of Special Education teachers and the instructional approaches they use to work with students identified with learning disabilities. Parents might also ask how the students with LD are performing on state assessments of reading and math. Finally, ask about the evaluation and eligibility process in your school district and get any printed information available for parents.

3. **Contact your state's Parent Training and Information Center (PTI).** Every state has at least one PTI, supported by funding from the U.S. Department of Education. Your PTI can help you understand the particular ins and outs of Special Education in your state. Ask for any printed information that will help you understand the process. There are also special PTI sites for military families. You can find a link to your state PTI on NCLD's *A Special Mother* Web page at www.ld.org/aspecialmother.

After you have done all this, you may feel the time has come to submit your request to the school. Here is a sample letter requesting an evaluation. (You can cut and paste this letter directly off the www.ld.org Web site.)

Your Name
Your Street Address
Your City and State
Your Phone Number

Date

Principal's Name
School Name
School Address

Reference: Student's Name
DOB: Student's date of birth
School: Name of School and enrolled grade

Dear XXXXXXX:

I am writing to you because my child is experiencing difficulties in school.

My child is having difficulties with XXX (provide detailed information on problems, including specifics such as grades, test scores, teacher comments, observations, reports from doctors, etc.).

For these reasons, I believe that it is crucial for CHILD'S NAME to be evaluated. I understand that you will send me an evaluation plan explaining the tests that may be given to my child. Once you receive my approval for the evaluation, would you please let me know when the evaluation will be scheduled?

I would also appreciate any other information you have regarding the evaluation, how eligibility is determined, and the general Individualized Education Program (IEP) process.

If you need more information, please call me at home (your home phone) or at work (your work phone).

Thank you very much for your kind assistance. I look forward to your prompt reply.

Sincerely,

Your Name
Your Contact Information

Please note that schools routinely perform screenings and other informal assessments to all students to help with their instructional programs. These schoolwide screenings do not require parental consent, and they are *not* to be considered an evaluation for Special Education. If someone in the school says, "Oh, we tested all the children in her class and everything is fine," that is not sufficient to rule out further evaluation. You still need to make the formal request, and the school needs your written consent to perform a formal evaluation.

When the school district receives your request, the administrators will decide whether or not to evaluate your child. They need to determine whether your child shows evidence of a suspected disability and whether there is sufficient evidence to call for an evaluation. In many cases, schools and school districts will have pre-referral intervention processes they will want to use, or may be required to use, prior to formal Special Education evaluation. (These were discussed in the previous chapter.)

Once you make the formal request, you should receive *written confirmation* of your request from the school district, along with a copy of your Procedural Safeguards, a document describing your legal rights and protections under IDEA. (You will find more about these Procedural Safeguards in the following chapter.)

It may sound a bit overwhelming, but with these early steps, and all the way along, keeping written records will be a lifeline to effective action, and even your own sense of control.

Let's take a short detour to talk about them.

Chapter 9

Records and Rights: Organizing Your Information

Y ou are entering a world in which organizing your records and understanding your legal rights are paramount. Your printer, your fax machine, and your mailbox may soon be working overtime, and you might very well feel that you are drowning in paperwork. If so, do not be tempted to get rid of the things you think you won't need. Trust me: you need everything. If you don't need it now, you might need it tomorrow, so keep everything—and I mean *everything*. It starts even before you request an evaluation. Recall in the sample letter in the previous chapter that you are instructed to "provide detailed information on problems, including specifics such as grades, test scores, teacher comments, observations, reports from doctors."

If you have not yet started to record your observations and concerns, now is as good a time as any to begin. Information about your child's school experience, evaluation results, meetings with teachers, counselors, specialists, administrators, and any decisions made regarding your child's education will be critical to your child's case and when making decisions that will most benefit your child.

Here are a few ground rules:

1. *Make a copy of everything.* Never rely only on an original, whether written by you or received from someone else. Originals can get lost or damaged. Keep the originals in a binder created for that purpose, and keep the copies in a sep-

arate binder or folder. And do not write on the originals! If you want to make notes on documents such as report cards or evaluations, make a copy and write on them—not on the originals.

2. *Create a Communications Log.* Make a record of *everything*. If you send an e-mail to a teacher, print out both the original e-mail and the reply and put them in the binder. If you receive a phone call, jot down the date and topic of conversation and as many details as you can remember. These are the types of things to record:

 • Records of meetings and their outcomes
 • Dates you sent or received important documents
 • Dates you gave the school important information
 • Dates of suspension or other disciplinary action
 • Notes on telephone conversations (including dates, person with whom you spoke, and a short description of the conversation)

3. *Do not rely on memory alone.* If you happen to meet your child's teacher in the hallway and you have a conversation about your child's progress (or problems), send a follow-up note thanking the teacher and reiterating the general points of the conversation. Sometimes the most important pieces of information are disclosed in such casual conversations.

4. *Keep your records in chronological order.* Don't just stick them in a file folder or binder any old way. If you do, you will quickly find it impossible to figure out if the meeting with Teacher A took place before the meeting with Reading Specialist B, or when Administrator C referred you to Counselor D. There is nothing worse than going into a meeting and being asked a question only to realize the answer is buried somewhere in that six-inch stack of unbound paper. I have found the best way to prevent this is to use tabs within a binder, separated into monthly (or yearly, or by grade) installments.

In addition, you will want to keep such things as:

- Report cards and progress reports
- Standardized test scores
- Medical records related to disability or ability to learn
- Awards received by the child
- Notices of disciplinary actions
- Notes on your child's behavior or progress
- Student handbook and policies
- Attendance records
- Samples of schoolwork

Eventually you will include the evaluation results and Individualized Education Programs (IEPs) and other official services plans such as 504 plans, but that is still a bit down the road.

All this record keeping may sound daunting, but many mothers have told me that it was the one thing in the entire confusing process that gave them a sense of control.

JOURNALING

In addition to keeping records, some mothers choose to keep a journal. This doesn't have to be specific to your child's progress in school or revolve around your child's challenges with LD. One mother told me, "I started a journal that I hope to give to my children someday. I record my thoughts and feelings, and talk about things that happen day to day. It's a creative outlet that allows me to focus on the positive as well as some of the more difficult things. To my surprise, I found this journal to be of immense help when it came time to talk about specifics in school meetings. I could go back and figure out exactly when things took place."

Chronology can be a daunting task. Every mother I talk to says things like, "He was first tested in kindergarten—no, maybe it was first grade—no, that's right, it *was* in kindergarten, but in the first half of the second year." So much happens in such a short space of time that it can be very difficult to put it all in its rightful place.

If you are so inclined, keeping a journal could be a nice way to organize your thoughts and record your actions. It has the added benefit of allowing you to sort through your own thinking and your own feelings. It forces you to slow down and gives you a clearer picture of all the progress you have made and the challenges that lie ahead.

Keeping a journal does *not* lessen or eliminate the need to keep organized records. A journal is purely optional and is meant to augment the records, not replace them.

Another important way to gain a sense of control is through knowledge. If you know what you are entitled to, and what the school should be doing to ensure you get the services your child needs, it makes things far easier when you actually make your requests. Otherwise you are at the mercy of the school. This may not be a bad thing, but it's better to *know* the school is doing the right thing, rather than simply assuming it is. And if they aren't, you'll be on much firmer ground if you can not only point this out but back it up.

The Parent Training and Information Centers mentioned earlier are a great place to start. That's what they are there for: to teach you about the rights you are entitled to under federal law. (You can find a link to the PTI Center in your state on NCLD's Web page, www.ld.org/aspecialmother.)

For now, let's focus on your rights as they apply to the formal evaluation.

PROCEDURAL SAFEGUARDS WHEN REQUESTING AN EVALUATION

A request for a formal evaluation is a powerful document. Without it, your child can continue to drift in the classroom, failing or falling behind, and you will continue to live in that "before the diagnosis" world of confusion and indecision. Once the request is received, it triggers a requirement for your school district to provide you with a copy of a notice known as the Procedural Safeguards Notice. This is a formal document that spells out for you all the rights and protections afforded both you and your child. The school is legally required to follow these safeguards in evaluating your child and providing Special Education services.

The Procedural Safeguards Notice must contain information about:

1. Your right to obtain an Independent Educational Evaluation (IEE) by a professional outside the school district *at public expense* whenever you disagree with an evaluation that has been conducted by the school. You are entitled to one IEE each time the school conducts an evaluation. The school district is required to allow outside evaluations, but is not required to accept the results. The "at public expense" wording can be a little tricky, so watch out. Generally, you must pay for this outside evaluation. Later, if it is determined that the school district's prior evaluation was inappropriate, you will be reimbursed for the cost of the evaluation. (Be sure to learn about your state or district policy regarding the IEE.)

2. Your right to *consent to evaluations* and to the school providing Special Education services. As mentioned before, the school district must obtain your written, informed consent before it can evaluate your child or begin to provide Special Education services to your child.

3. Your right to *see your child's educational records*, to have copies, and to have the records explained to you by school officials. If the records contain inaccurate or misleading information, you may ask that they be changed or make a written request for a hearing to challenge the information. School districts may release your child's records without your consent to other school officials or teachers who have legitimate educational interests in your child. They may also release records without consent in health or safety emergencies. If your child transfers to another district, the school district may release the records if you are informed that the records will be forwarded and have a chance to request the records and challenge any misinformation.

4. Your right to receive Prior Written Notice anytime the school district plans to evaluate the student, schedules a meeting where decisions will be made about the student's eligibility or educational placement, or refuses to evaluate or change the student's plan.

One father's story regarding Prior Written Notice is instructive.

PRIOR WRITTEN NOTICE:
LEARN FROM ALEX'S EXPERIENCE

Alex, the father of twin second-graders who attend elementary school in Delaware, told this story to the National Center for Learning Disabilities. Holly and Josh were born twelve weeks premature, which left them both with hydrocephalus as well as various learning disabilities. Alex began to participate in IEP (Individualized Education Program) meetings five years ago, when Holly and Josh were three years old. (We will talk about IEPs in chapter 14.) At each IEP meeting, Alex was given a small booklet that contained the Procedural Safeguards under IDEA.

"To be honest, I never actually read through it," Alex says. "I always trusted school staff and assumed that the teachers and therapists were doing all they could to meet my children's specific needs. The district staff never took the time to go over the Procedural Safeguards document with me, and I never realized exactly how important knowing your rights could be."

At his last IEP meeting, Alex was told that Holly had made only one month of progress in reading during the previous twelve months, and that she was falling farther and farther behind. During that meeting he asked for some additional intervention from the school reading specialist, but was told the reading specialist was already seeing too many children and did not have any additional time to spend with his daughter. The school staff told him that Holly would just have to make do with the small group instruction she was getting in the Special Ed classroom.

"I really didn't know what to say," Alex remembers. "Luckily, I talked to other parents and they recommended that I attend a seminar sponsored by our district's Special Needs PTA. A representative from our state's Parent Information Center was there, as well as two attorneys who explained, step by step, all the parent rights described in that little book that I had never read. It was there that I learned the three most important words that a parent of a child with disabilities needs to know: *Prior Written Notice*. I had heard district staff use this term once in a while, and thought that it only meant that the district had to give you ten days' notice before scheduling an IEP meeting.

"It actually means a whole lot more. At the Special Needs PTA meeting, I learned that *Prior Written Notice* means that when a school district *adds, changes, or denies* educational services to your child, they must explain to the parent *in writing* why the services are being added, changed, or denied. If the school district is denying you services, they most likely will not provide you prior written notice voluntarily—you will have to ask them to do it."

Alex took advantage of his state's Parent Training and Information Center and his school district's Special Needs PTA, and found them to be extremely valuable resources. "In my situation, the school district took our concerns more seriously when we requested them to give us Prior Written Notice concerning why my request for time with the reading specialist was being denied. The district ended up re-evaluating her reading skills and assigned a reading specialist to coach her teacher on how to better teach my daughter. It's not exactly what I wanted, but it's a start. I'm hopeful that the district will agree with me and get my daughter the additional help she needs. In the meantime, we are using a private tutoring service to supplement her instruction.

"I'm sure my story isn't all that unique, but I can't emphasize enough how important it is to know your rights under IDEA—especially those three words: *Prior Written Notice*. They can make some powerful things happen for you that might change the outcome for your child. Hang in there; you are not alone."

Prior Written Notice must also be provided if the school decides that there is not enough evidence of a "suspected disability" and, therefore, denies your request for an evaluation. As the name of this provision implies, the Prior Written Notice must be provided *in writing*, not by phone or a conversation in the school hallway. The Notice must include:

- A description of the action proposed or refused by the district

- An explanation of why the district proposes or refuses to take the action and a description of all student information used as a basis for the decision
- A statement that the parents have protection under the Procedural Safeguards
- Sources for parents to contact or to obtain assistance in understanding the various provisions of their rights under IDEA
- A description of other options considered and the reason why those options were rejected
- A description of the factors that influenced the district's proposal or refusal

At that point, you may go forward with your right to challenge the district's decision (we will cover this topic in a later chapter), but for now let's continue to focus on the evaluation. Specifically, what is it?

Chapter 10
"Does My Child Need Special Ed?": The Evaluation

The term *eval* has become a slang word in parent groups, the same way *meds* is used for medications. "We had the eval in the fall" is something you might hear one mother say to another, and if you do, you can be sure she is talking to another mother familiar with Special Education.

The first thing to know is that you need to be an active participant in planning for your child's evaluation. Do not submit your formal request and leave the rest up to the school without further involvement.

Here are some questions to ask to learn about the proposed evaluation plan:

1. What is the school district's time frame for completion of the evaluation? Is the time frame in calendar days or school days?
2. What do the proposed tests measure? In other words, what is my child being tested for? (The tests usually measure academic skill level in reading, math, writing, and spelling; intellectual ability; and speech or language development.)
3. Does the evaluation include a parent interview? (If not, see if they will include one. The interview gives you a chance to provide your own observations, express your concerns, and ask that your input be included in the evaluation report.)

4. Does the proposed evaluation address all of your concerns about your child? (NCLD has provided an online Worksheet for Organizing Your Concerns about School-Related Problems in their *IDEA Parent Guide*.)
5. How are the tests administered during the evaluation? Is this a good means of communicating with your child?
6. Who will do the evaluation and what specific expertise, training, and experience do they have with these particular assessments?
7. How soon after the evaluation is completed will the report be available?
8. How are the test results expressed, and what do they mean? Are they numeric scores, descriptive statements, percentiles, grade levels?
9. Will the results be explained in a way that is easy to understand? Do not overlook this! Test results can be notoriously difficult to decipher. (We'll hear from one parent about this very issue in the next chapter.)
10. Can I meet with the evaluator or school representative to discuss the results privately?
11. Will the evaluation results provide information to help develop specific recommendations about classroom strategies, teaching methods, and services and programs for my child?
12. What is the school district's process for amending or revising the evaluation report?
13. What is the school district's process for requesting an Independent Educational Evaluation (IEE)?

You will find the above questions listed on the NCLD Web site. You can print them out and take them with you to your initial evaluation meeting.

THE INITIAL EVALUATION

You have requested a formal evaluation, or the school has approached you with the recommendation that your child be evaluated. You have received your Procedural Safeguards Notice. You have provided written consent for the evaluation to proceed. Now it's time for the first, or initial, evaluation to determine whether your child has a disability that requires Special Education services.

The evaluation process includes a variety of tests to measure your child's academic skills, language skills, cognitive ability, and social and emotional status. These evaluations may include written observations of your child in the classroom (if the evaluation is for learning disabilities, then a classroom observation must be included).

If your child is found eligible for Special Education services, the information in the evaluation will be used to develop your child's Individualized Education Program, or IEP.

Many states have established time frames during which the evaluation must take place after you have provided your consent. (Question 1, above, covers this.) When you find out when, mark your calendar on the date your child's evaluation begins and on the date it should be completed. If your state does not have an established time frame, IDEA 2004 requires that the evaluation be conducted within sixty calendar days of receiving your consent.

The school district will provide you with an Evaluation Notice, that describes the tests the school proposes to conduct during the evaluation. Ask to meet with the evaluator or the school's Special Education administrator to discuss the proposed tests before the evaluation takes place. Ask what the tests will measure, and how and when they will be administered. According to IDEA, your school district must conduct an evaluation that uses a variety of different tests, procedures, tools, and strategies to gather the relevant information (this includes information provided by you). They can't rely on one single test; they need to use several. The requirements also state that your child must be evaluated in all areas in which a disability is suspected.

Take the time to learn about the various tests involved. The terms and jargon will drive you crazy, but do your best; and if you don't understand something, keep asking until you do. Use the list of questions provided to get those answers, and when asked, provide your own information about your child.

After you have reviewed the school's proposed Evaluation Notice, met with the evaluator, and asked all your questions, you will need to reach agreement on the proposed Evaluation Plan. You are perfectly free to object to certain tests or to require additional tests to be added to the plan. If you reject the plan, you will need to work with the school district to develop a more appropriate plan. If the school does not agree with your changes, you have the right to refuse your consent or begin an official dispute.

Do not take this lightly. These evaluation results will form the basis of some important decisions about your child's education.

PRIVATE EVALUATIONS

You may want to consider having your child evaluated privately at your own expense (or through your private insurance). If you do, be sure to make the school aware of the testing results so they will not administer the same tests within a short period of time, which will invalidate the results. It is important to note that you are not required to share those private test results. If, for example, you disagree with the private test results, you do not have to turn them over to the school. You can find qualified evaluators through advocacy groups and through private Special Education schools. Other parents in your school district may also know of reliable private evaluators. Generally, these evaluators can be found in university medical centers and children's hospitals. Before scheduling a private evaluation, you should review the credentials of the evaluator to make sure that:

- The evaluator meets your state's requirements (holds a state license)
- The evaluator will provide a detailed written report that includes recommendations for services that will address your child's needs
- The evaluator will provide you with a full, clear, and understandable explanation of the findings so that you can easily explain and support them when discussing the report with the school

- The school district generally accepts evaluations from this particular evaluator
- The evaluator is willing to attend school meetings to explain the results and reasons for the recommendations

TALKING TO YOUR CHILD ABOUT THE EVALUATION

Before we get too deep into facts and recommendations, let's take a short detour to remind ourselves who is truly at the center of all this activity and concern: your child. Of course, everything we're now talking about centers on the child's needs, but I am talking about the *child* now—not the child's learning style, not the child's difficulties in school, not the child's test scores. We can get so concerned with evaluations and meetings and who will be there and who will not that we may make our concern the central focus, rather than our child. If you are anxious or fearful about the evaluation, it's quite possible these emotions will rub off on your child, no matter how well you try to hide them. Do not assume he or she is unconcerned about the evaluation, and is not at all frightened or anxious.

Some mothers get so wrapped up in the process that they drag their son or daughter to doctor after doctor, meeting after meeting, with no preparation or explanation. Evaluations are given with the child in mind, and can even seem like a game—but for a child who picks up on *your* anxiety, it can be a little daunting.

Talk to your child. Be open and honest. Say something like: "The reason you are getting evaluated is so your school can figure out why learning is so difficult. It's going to show us and your teachers the best way to help you." Explain that the tests will include questions, puzzles, drawings, stories, and games, and not to worry so much about right or wrong answers, but to "do your best." A little explanation can go a long way toward reducing or even eliminating the fear and stress that in some cases could affect the results.

THE EVALUATION: WHAT IS IT?

No single test is used to determine whether a child has a disability or needs Special Education services. Several different formal and informal tests are administered, along with observations from the school and from the parents. In addition, a doctor, nurse, or other medical expert may be asked to provide information about your child's health and well-being.

The tests and measures should be selected based on your child's strengths, weaknesses, and the suspected disability. They measure the child's responses to a set of questions and are used to predict how well that child might perform in school.

The PACER Center, a Parent Training and Information Center in Minneapolis, listed the various types of tests available in an article for LD Online in 2007. (If you don't know about www.ldonline.org, do yourself a favor and visit the Web site, where you will find a wealth of informative articles about every aspect of learning disabilities.)

The PACER article lists the following important terms that parents may need to know when their child is to be evaluated for LD. A combination of some of these forms of testing will be used in an evaluation:

Curriculum-based assessments (CBAs) or curriculum-based measurements (CBMs). These tests are developed by school staff to examine the progress a child has made in learning specific materials that the teacher has presented to the class. They can be useful tools for teachers and parents in determining whether learning is taking place. They must never be used alone to determine whether a child is eligible for Special Education.

Standardized tests. Standardized tests are developed by experts for use with large groups of students. The tests are given according to specific standards. These tests assess what a child has already learned (achievement), or predict what a child may be able to do in the future (ability).

Norm-referenced tests. Norm-referenced tests are standardized tests that compare a child's performance to that of peers. They show where a child stands compared to other children of the same age or grade.

Criterion-referenced tests. These tests measure what a child is able to do or the specific skills a child has mastered. Criterion-referenced tests do not assess a child's standing in a group. Rather, they look at a child's performance measured against standard criteria. They may compare present performance with past performance as a way of measuring progress.

Group tests. Group achievement tests may not be used to determine eligibility for Special Education. Although they provide information about how a child performs compared to others of the same age or grade, they do not identify an individual student's strengths and needs. Only tests given individually to a child are useful in determining unique learning strengths and needs.

Schools look at many factors when selecting tests to use in an evaluation. Here are a few:
- Tests must be reliable. A test is reliable if it offers similar results when taken at different times or given by different evaluators. Parents may ask for the reliability of the tests given to their child if this information isn't discussed along with the test results.
- Tests must be valid. A test is valid if it measures what it was designed to measure.
- Tests must accurately reflect the child's aptitude or achievement. Standardized tests must have been validated for the specific testing purpose. They must also be given by trained and knowledgeable people.
- Tests and other evaluation materials must not discriminate against a child on a racial or cultural basis. They must be administered in a child's native language or other mode of communication unless it is clearly not feasible to do so.
- Factors such as a child's attentiveness, motivation, anxiety, and understanding of the test directions can affect the score.

Functional Assessment: Observations of the Child

Tests are an important part of an evaluation, but sometimes what children can do or need to learn is not reflected in their scores. A functional assessment looks at how a child actually functions at home, at school, and in the neighborhood. Functional assessment for some students includes looking at reading, writing, and math skills. For others, assessing whether the student is able to ride the city bus, dress without help, or handle money will be more appropriate.

Functional Behavioral Assessment

When a child has behavior problems that do not respond to standard interventions, a functional behavioral assessment (FBA) can provide additional information to help the team plan more effective interventions. A typical FBA includes the following:

- A clear description of the problem behavior
- Observations of the child at different times and in different settings. Observations should record (1) what was happening in the environment before the behavior occurred, (2) what the actual behavior was, and (3) what the student achieved as a result of the behavior.
- Behavioral interventions to address the behavior and teach behavior skills

Once a functional behavior assessment has been completed, the results may be used to write a behavior intervention plan or to develop behavior goals for the IEP.

WHO DOES THE EVALUATION?

The evaluation is conducted by a group of individuals. This group should include:

- You, as the parent or guardian. IDEA guarantees your right to be in on this evaluation. You know your child best and should be part of the evaluation process. There are many ways to participate, such as describing your child's strengths, sharing your dreams and goals for your child, and expressing your concerns.
- At least one of your child's general education teachers

- A Special Education teacher or special service provider related to your child's area of need (such as a speech/language therapist, physical therapist, occupational therapist)
- Someone from the school district who is qualified to provide or supervise Special Education services within the school

THE EVALUATION REPORT

After the evaluation takes place, using the tests and assessments listed in this chapter, the school district is required to provide you with a copy of the evaluation report. They are *not* required to provide it before the meeting that determines your child's eligibility for Special Education, however. *Ask the school district for a copy of the full evaluation report before any meetings so that you will have time to review it and prepare your questions.* Make your request in writing, and make clear your expectation to receive the report before any meetings.

Here is a sample letter you can follow (or, if you prefer, cut and paste from the NCLD Web site).

```
Your Name
Your Street Address
Your City and State
Your Phone Number

Date

Evaluation Team Leader
School Name
School Address

Reference: Student's Name
DOB: Student's date of birth
School: Name of School and enrolled grade
Dear XXXXXXX:

    Thank you for your assistance in preparing the
evaluation plan for my child. I look forward to com-
pletion of the evaluation and look forward to your
report. Would you please provide a copy of the
report to me as soon as it is available? This will
```

allow me sufficient time to review the results prior
to any meeting that determines my child's eligibility for Special Education services.

Thank you very much for your kind assistance. I
look forward to working with you and your staff.

Sincerely,
Your Name
Your Contact Information

Remember to add a copy of your letter, the reply, and the evaluation report to your Master file!

You can also request a meeting with the evaluator at the child's
school to get a complete review of the results so you can fully understand them before the Special Education eligibility meeting. This
informal meeting is not required by law, but it can be very helpful,
especially when confronted with the daunting task of figuring out
what on earth all those figures and percentages mean.

Let's take a look at that now.

Chapter 11
Interpreting the Hieroglyphics: Evaluation Results

W hen reading the previous chapters, and seeing the steps laid out in an orderly fashion, you might be lulled into a belief that everything will be smooth sailing. And for some mothers, that is exactly what happens: the evaluation is conducted, the mother receives the results, she attends the Special Education eligibility meeting, and her child moves on to get the necessary help. For other mothers, the path is the same but it's a rockier one, with a few unexpected obstacles along the way.

One such obstacle is the evaluation report itself, and the sometimes obtuse language that clutters it with jargon and indecipherable figures.

When you get the evaluation report, make two or three copies you can use as a work sheet and put the original in your Master file. Do not write on the original! Read the report several times all the way through, then read it again using a highlighter and making notes in the margins. Don't worry if you can't understand everything. Make a list of all the things you do not understand, and form each into a question.

Ask the evaluator to meet with you to review all these questions *before* the Special Education eligibility meeting. This is an informal meeting. Unlike the eligibility meeting, it is not required by law, though most schools will be in favor of an informal meeting, especially those who value collaboration with an informed parent. Even without the meeting, a school must still provide you with information you can understand.

I mentioned this issue in a discussion with Candace Cortiella, director of the Advocacy Institute and mother of a daughter with LD (see chapter 16 for the full interview). Candace told me, "It is very appropriate for a parent to say to a school, 'I need an opportunity to have an interpretive meeting about this evaluation before we go further in this process.' Parents should know that schools have an obligation to provide them with information that they can understand. I was fortunate in that my daughter attended a school district that was rather large and sophisticated, and that practice was routine. They wanted parents to understand the evaluation results. So parents should know that they have the right to ask for interpretations of test results in understandable terms."

Here are a couple more things to consider:

- If you have your child evaluated by professionals outside the school, this independent evaluation must be considered in decisions about your child's disability or educational needs (assuming you agreed with the private evaluation results; see chapter 10 for more information on private evaluations).

- When you go to the eligibility meeting, you are allowed to invite any person you want to the discussion of your child's evaluation results. Someone with special knowledge of your child or expertise in an area that would be helpful in understanding your child could certainly be a valuable addition to the team. Many mothers find it helpful (and comforting!) to have someone they know attend the meeting with them, such as a family friend, a relative, or an advocate from a local parent organization.

Now, having explained how things should work in an ideal world, let's hear from someone whose experience was not ideal.

Once she sent in her formal request for an evaluation for her son, Helen explained, "They contacted me and I filled out the forms giving my consent, and then they conducted the evaluation. After the eval, they set up a date for a meeting. A few days before that meeting they sent us the evaluation results, and they might as well have been written in a foreign language. I am educated, I have a law degree, and I had absolutely *no idea* what I was reading. A psychologist conducted one test. A reading specialist conducted another, a speech pathologist conducted another, and I pored over the results, all the while thinking, '*What* am I reading?' There were scores and percentages, but there was no interpretation. There was nothing to tell me what it all meant. In the back, they had three pages to explain the various scores and to break them down further, but it was all a foreign language to me. Before I studied law, I was an English major—I had no idea the English language could be so complicated and broken down into such small pieces. I must have read it a dozen times, and every time it seemed to become more obscure and confusing. I was overwhelmed.

"The evaluation contained no actual diagnosis, nothing I could point to and say, 'Ah, that's the problem.' It ended by saying something like, 'recommendations to be discussed at the meeting,' but because I had no idea what it all meant, I was completely unprepared for the meeting. I didn't know *how* to prepare! So I went to the meeting—my husband was there, the school psychologist was there, and the reading specialist was there. She was the one who helped me request the evaluation in the first place. She sat there, totally afraid to say anything. You could see it on her face. I could tell that she wanted to say something. Whenever I asked a question, she sat on the edge of her chair, obviously wanting to answer the question but nervous about it at the same time. Once again, it all came down to money. The system doesn't want to provide too many services.

"My husband, Jim, thought the meeting went really well—and so did I, because I didn't really know what Michael needed. The specialist told me, 'He needs this, this, and this,' and it all sounded reasonable. But then, at the end of the meeting, I asked, 'So what does this all mean? Does he have dyslexia?'

"They sat back and said, "Well, we're not diagnosticians.'

"I remember that clearly. I thought, 'Then what *are* you? If you can't give him a specific diagnosis, then what are all the tests for?' But again, I figured they must know what they're talking about. They seemed so confident in telling us what he needed, so we gave our consent. Now I wish I hadn't, because I would have gotten him help that summer. The problem was that I still didn't know what was wrong with him, so I didn't know what he needed. No one came out and said he has dyslexia or LD. Some of it worked out—he did need some of what they recommended, but he needed more intensive help.

"The bottom line is this: they gave us what they could afford, and as far as they were concerned, they gave me a lot. But that's not the point. It doesn't matter whether or not they felt they gave us a lot. If he needed more, I would have found him the help he needed. I would have paid for it myself.

"Michael still didn't have an official diagnosis. He was pulled out of class for reading, and he started getting one on one as well. He was making progress. He was getting small group instruction and some individual. All this time, I tried to figure out what was wrong. I bought books. I went online. I did everything I could to interpret the reports for myself.

"On top of all this, there was the hope that there might be nothing wrong with him at all. I think that is a *huge* problem with the system. Think back to the conference with the reading specialist, when I had to officially ask to have him tested before anything could be done. Many mothers are not going to ask. They want to believe that there is nothing wrong with their child. And think about the mother who is fearful, or not all that motivated to get involved in the LD issue. She might be working, a single mother—she's overwhelmed. I see it all the time. I've tried to help them, but some mothers just don't want to deal with it, or maybe they can't deal with it, so they don't ask for help. Think about it: the rent is late, you have three other kids, you're a single mother. Would you ask? Do you really want to hear about *another* problem?

"Teachers do help those kids along the best they can, but even so, they do not get the help they actually need. Sometimes the teachers have to push the parents into this because without that parent as a committed advocate, the child gets only minimal help from the reading specialist."

Try not to let Helen's experience become your own. If you do not understand the evaluation results, keep asking for an explanation until you get one. As Candace Cortiella reminds us, "Parents should know that schools have an obligation to provide them with information that they can understand." So try to put off any meeting that will determine a course of action for your child until *after* you ask for a meeting to explain the results of the evaluation.

For some mothers, this period after the evaluation and before Special Education services begin will be the first time they've had a "breather" since first suspecting their child had a problem. This is also the time when questions that have been put on hold begin to assert themselves. Primary among them is one that is notoriously difficult to answer: "What caused my child's learning disability?"

Let's try to answer it now.

Chapter 12

"Was It Something I Did?":
Causes of Learning
Disabilities

Around the time your child has been diagnosed with LD, you may find a disturbing set of symptoms arising within your own mind, usually revolving around the central question: "How did this happen?" For many, a second question follows closely behind: "Did it happen because of something I did?"

This second question really sets the gears in motion, and for some mothers, it can lead to years of guilt based on misplaced fears, misunderstood facts, or absolutely nothing at all.

When I was in Michigan recently for an LD-related event, a woman approached me and asked if we could talk privately. She had the look I know so well, the look that says, "I want to talk to you alone, and I don't want anyone else to hear us because I don't want anyone else to know." I moved away from the crowd and nodded to her, inviting her to come closer. She glanced over her shoulder as if someone might be following her, and then in a soft voice, she told me she had a daughter who had ADHD. "I've never told anyone about her ADHD," she said. "My daughter is grown, she's now a nurse, and I never told a single person outside the doctor's office until today."

"Why not?" I asked.

"Because I smoked when I was pregnant. I always thought it was my fault she had ADHD, and I was afraid to tell anyone."

I assured her that there are many causes of ADHD, and no one can pinpoint an exact reason why someone gets it. "If smoking was the single cause of ADHD or LD," I said, "it seems likely that nearly everyone born between 1925 and 1980 would have it! Don't beat yourself up over something in the past, *especially* over something that may not be true."

Almost every mother I've talked to about this has the nagging feeling that she did something wrong, even when she knows she didn't. I myself did not smoke or drink when I was pregnant (cigarettes and alcohol made me sick), but that did not prevent me from examining other behaviors in hindsight and asking myself if that may have been the cause. Did I eat enough? Did I eat too much? Why was I in labor so long?

Much of this is idle speculation on our parts. We're in a waiting room at the pediatrician's office, thumbing through a magazine, and suddenly—"I wonder if she didn't get enough oxygen when she was born? I was in labor for such a long time; I wonder if that caused it."

Lisa said of her suspicions and fears: "I didn't know I was pregnant until I was already five months along. I have always been athletic and paid attention to my diet. I kept my weight down when I was younger, so it wasn't unusual for me to not have my period. I was taking birth control and at one point I took antibiotics. I didn't know that taking antibiotics can lessen the effects of birth control. Five months later I was with some girlfriends in Vermont. I didn't know I was pregnant, let alone five months' pregnant. So we went rock-climbing, and I started to bleed. I thought it was my menstrual cycle, but I went to the hospital to check it out, and the nurse said to me, 'Do you want to hear the heartbeat?' I said, 'My heartbeat?' and she said, 'No, the baby's heartbeat.' *What?!*

"That's how I found out I was pregnant. I felt like I had *lost* five months. If I had known, I would have taken much better prenatal care, and so later, yes, it's true: I felt like I had caused all of my son's problems. I beat myself up so badly over this for so long, but as time went on and I learned more, I realized that I, too, probably have ADHD. So it wasn't the physical activity or discovering I was pregnant so late; it was the fact that I have ADHD that is the source of Ryan's problems."

Wondering what went wrong or what we may have done to contribute to our child's LD is understandable and possibly unavoidable, but the most relevant fact when considering the causes of LD is this: *no one really knows what causes LD, and in fact, there is frequently no apparent cause for LD.* There are contributing factors, but so far, science has been unable to pinpoint a single specific cause. Most researchers today believe that LD and related disorders are a result of subtle disturbances in brain structures and functions, disturbances that usually begin before birth.

The human brain is the most complex and sophisticated organ on the planet. It is made up of billions of interconnected nerve cells called neurons. A baby is born with more than 100 billion neurons, nearly all he or she will ever need. (Some scientists believe additional neurons are developed after birth, but those the babies are born with are the primary ones needed as they grow from children to adults.) In the early stages of pregnancy, the brain stem and midbrain form. These control the basic bodily functions necessary for life, such as breathing and digestion. Later a deep ridge divides the thinking part of the brain, known as the cerebrum, into two hemispheres, left and right. The last regions of the brain to fully develop are those involved in regulating emotions and abstract thought. Each region creates networks to help transmit information to other parts of the brain or body.

After birth, the brain continues to grow. By the time a child is three years old, the brain has reached 90 percent of its adult size. During this growth phase, the regions of the brain involved with learning are activated by information and stimulation, which provide the basis for learning. It's an amazing and miraculous thing, the human brain, so multifaceted and intricate that the greatest brains on the planet will never fully understand its workings. To me, the real wonder is how *few* problems there are, given how complex its development is.

Because it is so complex, things can sometimes go wrong. During pregnancy, the brain's development can be affected by the subtle disruptions mentioned earlier that affect the makeup or connections of the neurons. Some researchers believe these problems can show up later as learning disabilities. That's what we mean when you hear the phrase: "learning disabilities means the brain is wired differently."

Here are some of the things that can cause these disruptions:

- *Hereditary factors.* Learning disabilities often run in the family, so it is not at all uncommon to find that people with LD have parents or other relatives with similar difficulties. Entire families have been known to suffer from the same disorder, such as ADHD or anxiety disorder.

- *Problems during pregnancy and birth.* LD may be caused by illness or injury during or before birth. It may also be caused by drug and alcohol use during pregnancy, low birth weight, lack of oxygen, and premature or prolonged labor.

- *Incidents after birth.* Head injuries, malnutrition, and exposure to toxic substances (lead poisoning, for example) can contribute to LD.

Once again, I stress that most of the time there is no apparent cause of LD, and since no one can possibly know what caused it, mothers should try not to spend too much time wandering through the past, searching for a possible reason their child has a learning disability. There are far too many factors involved to allow anyone (including professionals) to pinpoint the exact cause with any certainty.

John, a Special Father (you will hear more from him in a later chapter), says, "LD is something that happens beyond everyone's control. But I think that many mothers feel some sort of responsibility because they delivered the child. Even if it was something inherited from the father's side, they still feel that. It's *their* child. And they seem to feel they did something wrong, even when the doctor tells them they didn't.

"In my case, my son's disability was the result of a random genetic event. It had absolutely nothing to do with anyone, but his mother still has a tendency to feel that she might have done something. But absent a situation like crack babies, where there is actual conscious behavior that obviously affects the child, the causes of LD are usually genetic. In some cases, neither parent had the gene—it's a random genetic event. But there are other cases where, clearly, the disorder could be passed on genetically from either side. But, having said that, I still think the mother tends to say, 'It must have been me.' Even if shown a gene study that clearly shows it came from her husband's side, she would *still* probably say, 'It must have been me.'"

Sometimes this acceptance of responsibility brings with it a burden of guilt that can be debilitating. I asked the women in the Special Mothers Club whether they ever had feelings of guilt or shame that they had somehow caused their child's disability.

"My mother was diagnosed with bipolar disorder," Dana said, "and I have an anxiety disorder. I am sure that's why my son has problems. I was convinced that it was all my fault, and so there I was one day, crying on the floor of my bedroom, apologizing to my husband for everything. It got very dramatic. I knew that the problems had come not from something I had *done*, but from who I *am*. It was in the genes, passed down from me to my son. That seemed to make it all worse, and I was devastated. It was something I always worried about because of my mother's problems. And, of course, you also worry if you're doing the wrong thing *now*."

Most mothers of children with disabilities tend to carry a certain amount of guilt, even when they know without question that they have no reason to feel guilty at all. Personally, it never occurred to me that I might be at fault when Allegra was diagnosed with LD. When she was a little older, though, I heard a pediatrician talking about the crack epidemic in the 1980s, saying that with the rise of crack use by the mother, we would soon see an overflow of children born with LD. That planted the notion that mothers could cause a disability, which started me on a cycle of self-blame.

It wasn't until I asked for a genetic test for Allegra that I learned that her LD was based on a chromosomal abnormality—a random genetic event attributable to no one. By this time Allegra was an adult, which meant I had already had about twenty years to stew in all the imagined things I had done or not done to cause her problems. Every time I did, I then thought, "What does it matter? It's not going to take away Allegra's problems." And that would satisfy me until the next unwelcome thought came to mind.

The best advice I can give is advice that I didn't always follow very well.

Let go of those feelings of guilt. What do they prove? Whom do they help?

We must try not to spend too much time in the past. We can visit once in a while, but let's try not to take so many souvenirs back with us. What's done is done.

Live in the present and do all you can now to help your child's future.

And this leads us to part III, in which I help guide you as you take your first steps into that maze we call Special Education.

PART III

After the Diagnosis

Chapter 13

Meetings, Meetings, and More Meetings!: Eligibility Determination

After the formal evaluation, decisions need to be made regarding a course of action. It all comes down to this question: based on information gathered in the evaluation, is your child eligible for Special Education services?

This is going to involve a meeting with the school, after which will be another meeting, and another meeting after that. This period of time will involve a lot of meetings, many documents, and the usual round of letters, e-mails, and phone conversations regarding attendees, most appropriate time, location, purposes of the meeting, and so on. As always, make sure you stay on top of things with well-organized record keeping and a file system.

This chapter will help prepare you for these meetings, using excerpts and adapted information from NCLD's *IDEA Parent Guide*. This guide explains the process, step by step, and with their permission, I now do the same for you.

First, though, let's talk a bit about meetings. It's one thing to read a list of the professionals who are required by law to attend the meeting with you and what is expected to take place. It's quite another to contemplate actually going into the room with these professionals without feeling a little intimidated or overwhelmed. Every mother I've talked to has gone into these meetings with a pounding heart and a fear that she might not know enough either to understand everything that is said or to challenge something she does not agree with. If you're lucky, your husband will be onboard and will attend all or most of the meetings with you. If not, try to convince him to come to the first meeting with you to provide moral support and a friendly face. Fathers really change the dynamics of these meetings. I strongly urge dads to attend, even if they don't contribute. But if your husband is not in the least friendly to the idea of Special Education, he may simply add to your fears—you be the judge.

The chances are good that many of you will be attending meetings not only with school personnel but also with pediatricians, psychologists, or neurologists brought onboard to help you understand what is going on with your child. Meetings can be enlightening during this time, or they can be traumatic. Listen carefully to what the experts tell you, but always realize that their pronouncements need not be considered the final word. If you hear something, anything, that sounds wrong or completely out of left field, do not hesitate to find a new doctor or to ask for a second opinion. If the school tells you things that don't make sense or it sounds as if they are talking about a child other than your own, make sure you do not leave that meeting until you feel you have fully understood their meaning and what they plan for your child.

Much of what you're told will probably be a little confusing in the beginning, but do not be intimidated. And do not face this alone. The law states that you are allowed to bring to the meeting one or more persons who have personal and/or professional knowledge of your child. This can be an outside private evaluator or tutor or an educational advocate. I asked Candace Cortiella, author of NCLD's *IDEA Parent Guide*, whether these people need to be professionals.

"No," Candace said. "It could be anyone. It could be your sister-in-law. That little dangling term is in the law to prevent people from bringing everybody they know. From the standpoint of the school, I would say they are guilty of this, too, but in the opposite way. They sometimes bring people into the IEP meeting who do not know the child at all. I had that happen to me personally. Still, it is good to be aware of the language of the law because the school would have the right to say to a parent who comes in with a nonprofessional, 'What is your relationship to this child?' But in general, they don't do that. Even so, it is best to prepare ahead of time. I have advocated that parents have an obligation to the school to let them know who they are bringing so that there are no surprises. Sometimes a mother might just want to bring her best friend Susie because Susie is going to take notes, and that's fine—but let the school know in advance."

Wouldn't these meetings go so much better for you if you took along someone you know and trust, someone who can provide that second set of ears to hear things you might otherwise not notice? Of course they would. So let's begin...

THE ELIGIBILITY DETERMINATION MEETING

After the evaluation process, the school must schedule a meeting to determine whether or not your child is eligible for Special Education services. This meeting may be called an *eligibility meeting* or an *initial IEP meeting*. IEP means Individualized Education Program—which we will cover in the next chapter, and which will become very familiar to you in the months and years ahead. Ideally, this should be a separate meeting, as it is happens *after* eligibility is determined. Some school districts may wrap the two issues into one meeting. Make sure you ask about this ahead of time.

The eligibility meeting must be scheduled for a time that is convenient for both you and the school staff. Although I would not recommend it unless absolutely necessary, this meeting may also be conducted from various locations by the use of technology, such as video-conferences or telephone conference calls. Even videoconferencing cannot fully replace the personal touch.

IDEA requires that the eligibility determination must be made by a group of qualified professionals, such as the school principal, school psychologist, Special Education teacher, general education teachers, and others involved in the evaluation process. The school will send you a written notice about this meeting and who will be attending. This group must include you (and/or your spouse) and the student's regular education teacher (or a "teacher qualified to teach a student your child's age"—this language is included in case the child doesn't have a regular education teacher). The group must also include at least one person qualified to conduct diagnostic tests, such as a school psychologist, speech-language pathologist, or remedial reading teacher. The law states that you have the right to bring other individuals to the meeting, provided that they have personal knowledge or special expertise regarding your child, such as an educational advocate, private evaluators, private tutors, or other professionals who have experience with your child, and, of course, a friend or relative for support.

Establishing eligibility under IDEA is a two-pronged process. Your child must meet the criteria of *both* in order to be eligible for Special Education services.

First, the student must be determined to have one (or more) of the thirteen disabilities listed in IDEA. These include autism, speech/language impairment, emotional disturbance, and SLD, or Specific Learning Disabilities.

Second, as a result of that disability, the student must need Special Education services in order to make progress in school and in order to benefit from the general education program.

Due to this two-pronged approach, it is possible that your child could be determined to have a disability such as a specific learning disability and yet not be in need of Special Education. In such cases, the student may be eligible for services under a category known as "developmental delay," which allows states to provide Special Education services to young children (ages three through nine) who are experiencing delays but do not meet the criteria for a disability category. This developmental delay category is a state option; many states do not use it.

Preparing for the Eligibility Determination Meeting

Ask Questions. The following list of questions should be asked *before* the meeting:

1. Will I be given sufficient time to review my child's evaluation report prior to the eligibility meeting?
2. If I have questions about my child's evaluation report, how will I get them answered prior to the eligibility meeting?

3. May I bring other individuals to the eligibility meeting with me? What is the school district's policy regarding nonschool attendees?
4. What is the school district's current policy regarding the determination of a specific learning disability?
5. If my child is found eligible, will the school district plan to develop the initial IEP at the same meeting?
6. If my child is found not eligible, will the school district consider an evaluation for eligibility under Section 504 of the *Rehabilitation Act?*

Section 504 of the *Rehabilitation Act* says that no one with a disability can be excluded from a public school education. A "504 plan" spells out the accommodations a student will need in order to perform at the same level as his peers (such accommodations could include use of a tape recorder, for instance). In the broadest sense, a 504 plan is a less intense form of the IEP. It tries to level the playing field to provide an opportunity for students with disabilities to perform at the same level as their peers. An IEP, on the other hand, is designed for students who need more than just an equal opportunity. These students require specially designed instruction in the classroom.

Gather Information. Go through your child's old and current records and look for things that will help your case, such as teachers' comments on report cards or notes or e-mails they may have written before your child was diagnosed. Bring your organized Master file along so you can quickly find the proper documents when you need them. There's nothing more frustrating than waiting for someone to pore through a pile of unorganized documents, searching for the right one.

Record the Meeting. A tape-recorded version of the meeting could be very helpful as you later try to recall the details. It's probably not a good idea to walk into the meeting with tape recorder in hand. You should first make a call to your state education department and find out if your state allows you to tape-record meetings. The state may say that they leave it up to the school district. If so, contact the district and request their written policy on recording their meetings. If they do allow it, most districts prefer that you notify them in advance if you plan to tape.

Personalize the Meeting with a Photo. This is certainly not required, but I think it's a good idea. One of our Special Mothers brings a framed photograph of her son to every meeting. She sets it out at the beginning so everyone can see who they are discussing. It makes it less likely for anyone to think of your child as a statistic or a faceless, generic student.

This is what will happen at the meeting. Someone will introduce all of the attendees. After this, the attendees will review the results of your child's evaluation. You should already have received a copy of the evaluation report before the meeting. If you did not receive it, you must be given a copy at the meeting—not the best time to receive it. The results are notoriously difficult to decipher, even with plenty of time to look them over. You will feel you are on much more solid ground if you have had a chance to review the report *before* going into the meeting. I urge you to request all reports in advance of any meeting.

The panel will also review any material that you want to include when determining eligibility. This may cover the results of private testing, reports from your pediatrician, or information from private tutors. As with the results of the evaluation, it is best that you provide this information to the school prior to the eligibility meeting.

A discussion will follow, taking into account everyone's views and the results of the various evaluations. When it comes to determining SLD, or Specific Learning Disabilities, federal IDEA regulations require them to determine that:

1. Your child does not achieve commensurate with his or her age in one or more of the following areas:
   • Oral expression
   • Listening comprehension
   • Written expression
   • Basic reading skill

- Reading fluency skills
- Reading comprehension
- Mathematics calculation
- Mathematics problem solving

2. Your child does not make sufficient progress in one or more of the above areas when provided with scientific, research-based interventions (such as those provided in a Response-to-Intervention process, as covered in chapter 7).

3. Your child exhibits a pattern of strengths and weaknesses in performance, achievement, or both (relative to age, state-approved grade-level standards, or intellectual development—for example, an achievement test shows a discrepancy between reading and math, indicating strengths and weaknesses in your child's academic skill level).

4. Your child has been provided appropriate instruction in reading or math.

5. Your child's lack of achievement is not primarily due to any of the following:
   - A visual, hearing, or motor disability
   - Mental retardation
   - Emotional disturbance
   - Cultural factors
   - Limited English proficiency
   - Environmental or economic disadvantage

The eligibility team also considers information acquired from observing the student to record academic performance and behavior in the areas of difficulty. These observations can be done prior to the formal evaluation, or can be conducted as part of the evaluation process.

Finally, the team must document its eligibility findings in writing. Each team member must certify in writing whether the written report reflects his or her conclusion and, if it does not, that member must submit a separate statement presenting his or her conclusions.

At the end of the meeting, a determination will be made about whether your child is eligible to receive Special Education services.

For Eligible Students

If your child is found eligible for Special Education, the next step is to draft a proposed Individualized Education Program (IEP) for your child. This IEP must be developed within thirty calendar days of the eligibility determination meeting. Special Education services cannot be provided until an IEP has been developed and you have provided informed consent.

As I mentioned, many school districts will combine the eligibility determination meeting with the initial IEP meeting, which can save time for all involved. If you prefer two separate meetings (my recommendation), let the school know ahead of time.

For Ineligible Students

If your child is not found eligible for Special Education services, you have the right to dispute the findings, as described in chapter 17.

You must be given documentation of the eligibility decision whether your child is found eligible for Special Education or not. As always, put a copy of this information in your Master file.

We will now tackle something you may have heard mentioned by someone you look upon as a veteran in the Special Education wars: the IEP. It is something that you, too, will become familiar with, as most of the skirmishes and conflicts that arise will take place over this document. Do not fear it, though! As with most things, knowledge is half the battle.

Chapter 14
IEP: The Individualized Education Program

Now that you have gotten through the eligibility meeting, you should gear up for what could prove to be the most challenging meeting of all—the IEP Meeting.

For those students found eligible for Special Education services, the next step is to develop an IEP, or Individualized Education Program (sometimes called an Individualized Education Plan). Consider the IEP your blueprint of which Special Education services will be provided to your child. The word *individualized* in the title of the program means that it must be tailored to your child's needs—not to the needs of the school district, or a teacher, or a specific classroom, or even a child *like* your child. *Your* child. The school cannot say, "We know your child needs this particular accommodation, but we don't do that in this school." Too bad. If your child needs that accommodation (and if a similar accommodation that leads to the same results is not available), then the school must provide it.

The IEP is a legally binding document that includes your child's classification, placement, type of services required, academic goals, behavior goals and a behavior plan (if needed), the percentage of time your child will spend in regular education, progress reports from teachers and therapists, and input from you, the parent.

An IEP must be developed within thirty days of the eligibility determination meeting. It must then be reviewed annually as long as the student is eligible for Special Education services (which also means you will take part in a yearly IEP meeting for the same length of time). These services cannot begin until an IEP has been developed, and that is what happens in an IEP meeting.

THE IEP MEETING

As mentioned earlier, some school districts will suggest including the initial IEP meeting at the same time as the eligibility determination meeting. If this appeals to you, by all means take advantage of it. If you would rather wait for a separate IEP meeting, however, let the district know in advance of the eligibility meeting and it will schedule a second meeting for a later date. I would recommend separating the two meetings. At the first meeting, you will be anxious about the results and either relieved or disappointed by the findings. I do not think that is the best time to go into the details of an IEP plan. You need time to do some research. You need to sit down and think through your goals for your child, and you can't do that only minutes after finding out your child is entitled to the services.

The school district is required by law to make sure that one or both parents are present at every IEP meeting. They cannot call you and say, "We've scheduled it for an hour from now, hope you can make it." They must send *written notice* of the meeting early enough to ensure you have an opportunity to attend, and they must schedule the meeting at a mutually agreed upon time and place. As with the eligibility meeting, you may conduct this meeting using technology such as videoconferencing, and as before, I do not recommend this unless absolutely necessary.

The school is required to send you a written notice of every proposed IEP meeting. They will do this via e-mail or regular mail. The notice must state the purpose of the meeting, the time and location, and who will attend. It must also inform you of your right to bring other individuals to the meeting. In theory, the school can conduct a meeting on its own, but this happens only when it has documented proof of having tried repeatedly to involve the parents. Sadly, there are some parents who do not take an interest, and we should all be thankful that the schools step in to help.

Preparing for the Meeting

Preparing for a meeting can be challenging and even nerve-racking, mostly due to the unknown. *Will I know what to say? What if I ask for the wrong things? Will I feel like everyone knows so much more than I do?* This is all new to you. You have entered unknown territory, so it is quite natural to feel dislocated and off-balance. This is why I hope you will separate the eligibility meeting from the IEP meeting (or any other meeting). You need time to gather your thoughts and collect yourself. The best way to do this is to prepare as best you can for the unforeseen.

The first thing to do is go online and visit Web sites such as NCLD's www.ld.org and www.LDonline.org, or those of the Learning Disabilities Association of America (www.ldanatl.org) or the International Dyslexia Association (www.interdys.org). (You will find these organizations listed in our Resource Directory at the back of this book.) Do your research. Talk to other parents who have already been through it.

On the night before the meeting, collect all the information you have gathered and make notes on what you would like to say at the meeting. Don't expect to remember your questions—you will surely forget at least one of them. Write them down. Review the contents of the Master file you have created for your child. Look over the contacts you have had with school personnel regarding your concerns about your child's progress in school.

Finally, look over the list of people who will attend the meeting, also known as the IEP team.

The IEP Team

Those present at the meeting will make up the IEP team. These include:

- You and/or your spouse
- One of the student's regular education teachers
- At least one Special Education teacher
- A representative from the school district who is qualified to provide, or supervise the provision of, specially designed instruction and is knowledgeable about the district's resources

- An individual who can interpret the instructional implications of the evaluation results (this may be a school psychologist or one of the teachers or the district representative listed above)
- Any individuals who have personal knowledge or special expertise regarding your child, such as an educational advocate, private evaluator, private tutor, or other professional who has experience with your child (this may also include the person you brought along to the earlier meetings who can be your source of support, even if he or she acts only as your note taker)
- The student (if and when appropriate). You should talk to members of the IEP team ahead of time to determine whether your child is old enough to be part of the IEP team meeting.

Be sure to read the meeting notice to make sure that all these members will be at the meeting and that they will be available for the entire meeting. If you have any concerns about the attendees, make sure you contact the school in writing about this ahead of time.

Sometimes the school district will try to exempt one of the members from attending the meeting, usually for legitimate reasons. The law provides two ways that the team members can be excused from attending the meeting, in whole or in part:

1. If the member's area of the curriculum or related services is not being modified or discussed, or
2. If the member's area is being discussed and that person has submitted written input to the parents and the team before the meeting.

In both cases, parents must provide written consent for the member to be excused. This applies even if the team member wants to be excused from only part of the meeting. If you prefer that the school district not excuse any team member, you need to notify the school in writing in advance of the meeting. This puts the school on notice that you will not agree to any absences (unless you are notified in advance and agree to them). They cannot announce that "So-and-so couldn't make it" at the beginning of the meeting. They have to tell you ahead of time and request your agreement.

What Happens at the IEP Meeting

The meeting will usually take place at the school, either in a classroom or a conference room. You will come in with all your notes, your Master file binder, copies of any article you would like to distribute, a tape recorder (if allowed—be sure to ask ahead of time), and, it is hoped, an optimistic attitude. Try to summon a positive attitude, especially for this first meeting. There may come a time when such a thing is a challenge, but for now, go in with the expectation that things will go your way.

Another point I would like to stress is your personal presentation. Fashion might be the last thing on your mind on the day of the meeting, but give it some thought. How you dress will show how seriously you take this meeting. I am not advising you to show up in an evening gown and jewels. I am simply saying it is not advisable to show up looking as if you just came from the gym or painting the basement. Present yourself as the mother you are: someone with a deep and serious interest in her child's education. Think of it as a business meeting—because it *is* business. The district personnel attending the meeting certainly think of it that way, and so should you.

How the meeting will progress is so dependent on the personalities of the people involved and the nature of the issues discussed that I cannot possibly give you a summary of a "typical" meeting. Some will go smoothly. Some will have bumps along the way. Some of the school officials will be understanding and helpful; others may obstruct or try to intimidate you. Some will view your child as a person with individualized needs. Others will think of your child more as a statistic (a photo of your child on the table before you, as mentioned earlier, can help alleviate this cold, bureaucratic way of thinking).

Regardless of how the meeting goes, you can be sure that next year's IEP meeting will not be the same. Nor will you be the same. You will have gained experience and knowledge. Sometimes it helps to realize that the reason some IEP meetings get more contentious over

the years is because the parent becomes more confident, more knowledgeable, and better equipped to get what she wants.

IEP Forms

Most school districts and/or states have developed IEP forms,
which must contain all the elements required by the federal IDEA law.
They may also contain elements unique to your state or school district. If your school has developed one of these forms, try to get a copy
before the meeting so you can review it beforehand and mark those
places you might not understand.

Bear in mind that some of these forms can limit your flexibility
when it comes to providing details about your child that you feel are
relevant and important. Don't feel bound to rigid guidelines. If the
school's IEP form does not provide a place for information you feel is
important, bring up your concerns at the meeting. Don't worry about
whether the form provides enough space for the information you would
like to include—include it anyway, on a separate sheet of paper if necessary. The needs of the students need not conform to the IEP. On the
contrary, the IEP must be tailored to the student's individual needs.

DEVELOPING THE IEP

Several components must be considered when developing the IEP.
Let's review them one at a time.

Consideration, or Primary, Factors

These are the main factors that must be looked at and discussed
when developing your child's IEP. These are:

- Your child's strengths
- Your concerns for improving your child's education
- The results of your child's initial evaluation or most recent
  evaluation
- The academic needs of your child
- The developmental and functional needs of your child

The IEP team (including you) will consider each of these factors,
which will help the team develop a statement about your child's pres-

ent levels of academic and functional performance. Your input is vital. Your concerns are as important as those of the school, so you should be prepared (ahead of time, if possible) to provide a written statement of those concerns.

For instance, if you are concerned about your child's reading ability, make sure you put that in your statement. Your concerns about your child's developmental and functional needs will help the other team members create an IEP that reflects those concerns. (When we include "developmental and functional needs" as one of the factors considered when developing an IEP, we mean such things as problems with attention, social skills, behavior, and all other areas of development that can influence your child's academic performance.)

Special Factors

After the Consideration Factors have been reviewed, the IEP must then consider a list of Special Factors that might require additional elements in the IEP, such as language needs for a child with limited English proficiency or a child who is visually or hearing-impaired. These Special Factors also include the need for assistive technology devices for children with disabilities, such as calculators or special computer software.

A final Special Factor involves behavior, specifically "the use of positive behavioral interventions and strategies to address a child's behavior when that behavior affects his or her learning." In other words, if members of the IEP team feel that a particular child's behavior is interfering with learning, they should develop a behavior intervention plan as part of the IEP. (This is an admittedly wide area for discussion and should be of concern only if your child's behavior adversely affects his or her learning. The Center for Effective Collaboration and Practice has developed a Web site devoted to Functional Behavioral Assessment that can be found at http://cecp.air.org/fba/default.asp.)

Present Level of Performance

This section of the IEP is a statement about how your child is doing now. The Present Level of Performance, or PLOP (sometimes known as the less amusing PLP), should be a detailed and accurate statement of your child's present level of academic and functioning performance. This statement is drawn from a variety of information and data (including information provided by you) and is a very important component of the IEP. After all, if we don't know where the child is now, how can we tell where he or she is supposed to be? Provide your own input, and if you feel the other team members are either minimizing or exaggerating your child's current abilities, be sure your objections are included in the IEP. The performance statements should also be as detailed as possible. NCLD gives the following examples of inappropriate vs. appropriate statements:

Inappropriate: Susan is not progressing adequately in the second-grade reading curriculum.

Appropriate: Susan is reading 15–20 words per minute with three to eight errors in second-grade material. She reads slowly with inaccurate decoding skills.

See the difference? The first is generic and vague, more of an overview of a problem compared to the specific, pinpointed information in the second. If something sounds like it could be said about any child having trouble in school, ask the team to be a little more specific.

Measurable Annual Goals

The IEP team then develops a set of measurable annual goals, which should focus on the knowledge, skills, and strategies required to address the student's needs resulting from his or her disability. In other words, these goals should not list everything the student is expected to learn in every class, including those unaffected by the particular disability. The question should be: "What does the child need to better help him or her master the schoolwork?" rather than "What is the schoolwork the child needs to master?"

For example, if your child has trouble reading essays in geography class, the goal should be to improve overall reading skills, rather than the more specific goal of knowing the various regions in France. At the same time, the effort to improve overall reading skills should be specific and well defined. It is not enough to say there will be improvement in an area of learning. How much improvement? Let's use another set of inappropriate and appropriate goals as an example.

Inappropriate: Susan will improve her decoding skills and reading speed.

Appropriate: Susan will read 80 words per minute with zero to two errors in second-grade material.

This may seem overly specific, but it is not. We will need a way to measure Susan's improvement in reading speed. If we are specific with Susan's Present Level of Performance, we must also be specific with her Measurable Annual Goals or we'll never get an accurate picture of her progress.

Progress Reporting

The IEP team will next specify how your child's progress toward meeting the annual goals will be measured and reported to you. IDEA states that the IEP must contain a description of how your child's progress toward meeting the annuals goals will be measured and when the school will provide you with reports concerning that progress. Some schools will issue quarterly reports, which will be sent at the same time as your child's report cards.

Ideally, these progress reports should be stated in objective, meas-urable terms such as those listed in the *appropriate* example of the Measurable Annual Goals ("Susan will read 80 words per minute"). These are concrete numbers or scores, establishing what the IEP team considers an acceptable level of performance or progress.

Services/Programs

Every service your child will need to accomplish the annual goals should be listed in the IEP. This includes such things as one-on-one aides, resource rooms, extra time for tests, reduced homework, and so on. *The school is obligated to provide whatever services, supports, and accommodations the IEP team includes in the IEP.* This is very important, and one reason why it can be very helpful to bring a tape recorder. If a member of the team says your child should have a one-on-one aide and everyone agrees but no one writes it down, you can't later say, "Well, I think I remember that someone said it." Get them to put it in the IEP then and there.

This statement of Special Education services must include specif-ic information such as:

- Dates. When services will begin and end (generally one year).
- Location. Where the services will be provided. Special Education instruction must be provided to students with disabilities in what is known as the least restrictive environment. IDEA includes provisions that ensure that children with disabilities are educated with nondisabled children, to the maximum extent appropriate.
- Frequency. How often services will be provided—for example, the number of times each day or number of days each week.
- Duration. The period of time each service will be provided.

Therapies and Related Services

In addition to the Special Education services, the details of any speech or physical therapy your child receives should be included in the IEP, with the same clear and measurable goals as the Special Education services, and details of frequency and duration of these therapies. *Related services*, as defined by IDEA, means "transportation and such developmental, corrective, and other supportive services as are required to assist a child with a disability to benefit from Special Education." These services include things such as speech-language pathology and audiology services, psychological services, and physical and occupational therapy. Parent training can also be a related service.

Participation in General Education

The IEP team must state the percentage of your child's day that will be spent in a regular classroom and the percentage of time spent in Special Education away from children who do not have a disability. As you'll see in my interview with Candace Cortiella (in chapter 16), many parents find this issue the most frustrating and challenging of all. They feel their child is being shuffled off to the side or completely segregated from his or her peers. This requirement on the IEP is designed to protect your child's right to be educated in the least restrictive environment as required by IDEA.

Accommodations and Assessment Participation

The IEP team will develop a statement about any individual accommodations that your child should use while taking state- and districtwide tests or assessments, including those required by the *Elementary and Secondary Education Act* (known at the time of this writing as the *No Child Left Behind Act*. This will undoubtedly change with the next reauthorization).

Your Comments

If you want the IEP team to know anything particular about your child's background, make sure you put it in the IEP. As mentioned earlier, if the IEP form does not include a space for parents' comments, ask the team to add space. If your concerns are in the IEP, they cannot later say they were never told. Sometimes the space will be filled in with comments you made at the meeting. That's fine, if you agree with it and the comments cover all the points you would have made. If you disagree with anything and want to put those disagreements on record, write them up and ask that they be included in the comments section. This is your opportunity to lay out those details about your child that only you might know, and which may have some bearing on his or her success in achieving the goals of the IEP.

FINALIZING THE IEP

After the team has developed the IEP, you and the other team members will be asked to sign it. Your signature is your informed consent for the school to begin Special Education services. These services should begin as soon as possible after the IEP is signed.

Do not feel pressured to sign the IEP at the meeting. You can ask to bring it home to review before you sign. Use the following NCLD checklist as you review the IEP to make sure it contains all the required elements. (You can also print out this list from the Web page: www.ld.org/aspecialmother.)

- Is the information in your child's Present Level of Performance clearly stated and supported with objective information and assessment or evaluation data, such as information from standardized testing, curriculum-based measurements, or performance on district- or statewide assessments?

- Does the Present Level of Performance section of the IEP contain information about the academic, developmental, and functional needs of your child?
- Are your concerns and expectations for your child included in the Present Level of Performance section of the IEP?
- Are your child's annual goals clearly stated and can they be measured?
- Knowing the effects of your child's disability, do the annual goals directly relate to your child's needs as stated in the Present Level of Performance?
- Is the specific way(s) to master the annual goals clearly stated?
- Is the method(s) to monitor and evaluate your child's progress toward the annual goals clearly stated?
- Does the IEP indicate the amount of time your child will spend in general education?
- Are the Special Education services and related services recommended for your child supported by scientific research that supports their effectiveness? If not, what evidence has the school provided to indicate that the services and instructional methods proposed for your child have been found to be effective for children with similar learning difficulties and of similar age?
- Does the IEP state who will be responsible for implementing the services listed?
- Are the appropriate related services addressed on the IEP?
- Do you know how the IEP content will be communicated and shared with the staff responsible for their implementation?
- Are all of the appropriate accommodations listed?
- Does the IEP indicate how your child will participate in state and district testing?
- Have any potential consequences of your child's assessment participation been explained to you?

- Have you discussed whether your child may or may not be allowed to move on to the next grade or graduate with a regular diploma?

If you accept only parts of the proposed IEP, indicate which parts you accept and which you do not. Provide a written explanation of your disagreements, which can be included as an addendum to the IEP. A second IEP meeting may be scheduled to go over these disagreements.

If you refuse to accept the IEP in its entirety, indicate your refusal on the IEP form. You may still be asked to sign it, but be sure that your signature in this case indicates only that you were present at the meeting and not that you are giving your consent to the services outlined in the IEP. This refusal is not to be taken lightly, or done on a whim because you didn't like someone's attitude in the meeting. It should happen only if you truly feel the services offered are inadequate or detrimental to your child. Refusal to sign the IEP gets into the area of Dispute Resolution, which will be taken up in a later chapter. If you do not give your informed consent, the school cannot and will not begin Special Education services.

A FINAL WORD ABOUT THE IEP

The IEP is such a large, complicated subject that it could be (and has been) the subject of an entire book. I have given an overview, but strongly urge you to do further research on your own. The whole process can be frustrating and confusing, but it really is the foundation of your child's Special Education experience. I look at Allegra's IEPs from years ago and still find them daunting, but I have kept them all as documents that formally measured both her successes and areas for improvement. Each one is a building block that aided her progress toward her goals. The same will be true for your child.

Knowing this doesn't always make the experience any easier. In the next chapter, we will hear from one of our Special Mothers whose initial encounter with her school's Special Education services was less than ideal, but unfortunately not that uncommon

Chapter 15
A Mother's Frustrations, a Mother's Solutions

It is all well and good to offer guidance and advice about the best way to deal with school bureaucracy, but sometimes the reality of the process seems far removed from the "official" advice. It's a little like walking down stairs: I could give you page after page of advice on the ideal, most practical way to descend a staircase, but if you have tripped over a neglected toy at the top and you're on your way down, you may discover your experience less "ideal" than the ones I'd described to you.

Sometimes experts focus so much on the way things *should be* that they lose sight of the way things *are* for some mothers. "But that's not how it's supposed to be," they tell me, and insist that these are isolated incidents. When I hear mothers talk about these various isolated incidents of conflict with a school, I won't say it indicates a trend or is in any way typical for most mothers, but it would be a disservice to discount them.

Much of this conflict with schools and school personnel stems from our own ignorance of what is expected from the school and what is expected from us. I have talked to many mothers whose early days with LD were shrouded with uncertainty and fear, but who were able to acquire enough knowledge to dispel those fears and gain control of the situation.

One such mother is Helen. You met her in earlier chapters when she discovered that her son Michael couldn't rhyme and later spoke of her bewildering ordeal when she tried to have him evaluated. Her story may not match your own in its particulars, but I have no doubt that many of you will relate to her frustrations. If the process has been smooth sailing for you, congratulations! If not, I hope you will benefit from Helen's solutions and advice in this chapter so you can pass from a sense of frustration to one of control. I follow this chapter with an interview with an advocacy expert who sheds light upon many of the situations faced by Helen and other mothers whose frustration with the school system has reached the boiling point.

HELEN'S PATH: "AS DIFFICULT AND INEFFICIENT AS POSSIBLE"

Helen's son Michael was eventually diagnosed with dyslexia. We last spoke with her about her meeting with the school officials concerning Michael's evaluation. At the end of the meeting, the officials acknowledged that her son had a problem with reading, but would not offer a specific diagnosis of dyslexia or learning disability. "So what does all this mean? Does he have dyslexia?" Helen asked and was told, "Well, we're not diagnosticians."

"I remember thinking," Helen says, "'Then what *are* you? If you can't give him a specific diagnosis, then what are all the tests for?'"

"If you had gotten an official diagnosis of LD that day, then what?" I asked.

"We could have moved on and dealt with it," Helen told me. "But with such vague answers, I couldn't tell what was wrong, so I didn't know what he needed. I trusted them. And some of it worked out. He did need some of what they recommended, but he needed more intensive help."

"Why didn't they give him what you think he needed?"

"They gave me what they could afford," she said. "It's expensive, and as far as they're concerned, they gave me a lot. I did have him evaluated independently, but that came later. Back then, at the beginning of the evaluation process, I believed everything they said."

"When did all this take place?" I asked.

"In first grade. After the evaluation, Michael had been pulled out of class for reading, and he started getting one-on-one instruction as well. They did a good job with that. He was getting the services he needed and he was making progress, so I thought everything was going the way it should. He still didn't have an official diagnosis, but even so, he was getting small group instruction and some individual instruction. All during this time I was buying books, and going online, and doing everything I could to interpret the evaluation reports for myself."

"Did you assume your son had dyslexia?"

"No, not at all! They had to give him an official label of having a 'specific learning disability,' but then they turned around and never said he actually had LD."

"Why would they do that?"

"They had to give him an official label in order to get him on an IEP. They called it a 'specific learning disability,' which is one of the allowable categories in the process to put a child on an IEP. The trouble is, they made it sound like it was merely a technicality to get him a little help. They didn't give any sense of urgency, or even of it being a legitimate issue. When I asked what the specific learning disability was, they said they would call it a reading disability. They wouldn't call it dyslexia—in fact, that's when I asked if it was dyslexia and they told me they couldn't answer because they weren't diagnosticians. I didn't know they were avoiding the term dyslexia on purpose, so I went with reading disability. It sounded fine to me. It also allowed him to be put on an IEP—and that was another nightmare to understand."

"In what way?" I asked.

"The form is impossible, especially for someone new to it all. I could barely interpret it. They show what they're doing now and what they need to be doing, and I thought, 'Okay, I'm not a teacher, how am I supposed to know if this is really what he needs?' Now that I know so much more, I look at that older IEP and I think, 'How did I ever let that go?' It was so vague. I finally took it to someone who knew a little more than I did at the time, and that person said, 'This is not acceptable.' Before then, I thought it was just me. I was intimidated, too, and insecure in my own knowledge and abilities. I didn't know what the forms were supposed to say. So I assumed my son was getting the help he needed."

"Was he?" I asked.

"In first grade, yes. And the summer after first grade, he qualified for summer tutoring, though once again it all came down to the fact that I had asked for it. I didn't know I had to ask for it to get it, but after my earlier experience with the evaluation, I now assumed I needed to ask for everything and that most things would not be freely offered."

"And if you hadn't asked?"

"I wouldn't have gotten it. But for that summer, he did get one hour a week with a tutor provided by the school. When September came he had to transition to second grade in a new school. It was too bad that he had to transition to a new school, because it was much bigger, with kids up to fifth grade. Everything changed. The classrooms changed, and he had to be in the schoolyard with all these huge kids. And, financially, that school is in pretty bad shape. The Special Ed people at the school told me that they were going to handpick a teacher for him. They chose one that everybody raved about, so I was relieved and assumed everything was going according to plan and in my son's best interest. They put him in what they call a 'collaborative classroom.'"

"What does that mean?"

"It means a classroom that has children with and without special needs," Helen said. "It is very similar to a mainstream classroom. In fact, they don't really come out and call it a collaborative classroom at all—they only do that behind the scenes. Officially it's a mainstream classroom that's a little more inclusive than most. It has a wide array of students, both regular and Special Ed. They have a regular teacher and a Special Ed teacher in the same classroom. They don't segregate the children with special needs. Of course, it's not popular with everyone. A lot of parents whose children do not have a problem do not want their children in the same class as those children with a disability. That made it very hard for me when I had to tell them that Michael is one of 'those children.'"

"How did you feel when you told them?" I asked.

Helen shook her head, as if still struggling with the emotions of those early days. "I remember the moment exactly," she said. "I was at a party and a friend was talking about a boy we knew and said, 'Jason is in *that* class.' She was making fun of him, and making fun of the children in *that* class. I was horrified."

"Did you say anything?"

"Yes. I was irritated by the way she was talking about it, so I looked at her and said, 'My son is in that class. He's one of those kids you're talking about.'"

"What did she say?"

"Nothing. She just froze. She didn't know what to say. That night when I went home, I had such anxiety. I couldn't sleep. I spent the night thinking, '*Why* did I say anything? Why did I tell them?' And, of course, I felt terrible that I was ashamed of that."

"Of course!" I said. "I went through the same thing. I think every mother goes through it at some time or other. You feel embarrassed or ashamed, and then you feel so guilty for feeling those things."

"Right. I remember lying there thinking, 'Who are they going to tell?' and then I felt guilty for thinking that way. It was awful. I didn't want everyone to know about Michael's disability. I went through a time when I wanted to keep it completely private. In fact, there are still people I don't want to tell, because I don't want to label him, even though I now find that most of the labeling comes from the teachers, not from other parents. For instance, my son had reading problems, but they also put him in a Special Ed math class, and there was no reason for that. He's great at math!"

"So you believe the teachers labeled him?"

"Yes. They did it by making assumptions about him, and once you are put in those classes, all the other kids assume you need special help for math. People can be judgmental—both children *and* their parents—so it's a difficult thing to figure out who to tell and who not to tell. As I said, even now there are certain people I would never discuss it with. On the other hand, I meet people who obviously need help with their own child, and I have no hesitation about sharing my story with them."

"So what happened with Michael in the new school?"

"He's in this school, in second grade, where everyone is raving about the teacher, and then comes the fall Open House, when all the parents go in and meet the teachers and see the classroom. Remember, the Special Education experts handpicked this teacher who everyone assured me was terrific—and she probably is, in most cases. I went into that Open House expecting great things, but it quickly became clear that this teacher didn't know a thing about my son. She didn't even know who he was. She was supposed to be his teacher, but she had almost no contact with him. He wasn't her problem. She wouldn't even talk with me, but pushed me off onto another woman who was the Special Ed reading teacher. She told me how Michael was doing with his reading and what she was doing with him. Then she told me he was getting pulled out of the collaborative mainstream class and put into a special room off the library with ten kids for an hour and a half of reading.

"There was no collaborative classroom, as I had been told. No mainstreaming at all. I wasn't really alarmed by the news, though I wasn't completely happy, either. Only later did I find out that this group of kids included children who were extremely disruptive and were put there because they were out of control. These disruptive kids didn't have a reading disability at all, even though that's what the class was supposed to be for. They shipped them off out of the way and put them all together in that little room off the library."

"And you didn't know any of this."

"No! I was involved with the school at that time, and I kept making requests to go visit that class, but they wouldn't let me. They said it was a privacy issue. I offered to sign a paper to say I wouldn't say anything about the other students."

"How did you eventually find out what the class was like?"

"Michael told me. He doesn't divulge information right away, so I had to pry it out of him, little bits and pieces here and there. And then I found out more on my own. It wasn't too long before I realized that the class that was supposed to help him in the area he most needed help wasn't helping at all. He wasn't learning a thing. And for math class—as I said, he was terrific in math. Sometimes he would do simple math problems on his own for fun. I assumed he was in the regular math classroom. Why wouldn't he be? It should have been clear to everyone that he could do the work. But no, that was not the case.

"He had been tutored in the summer by a teacher who had been transferred over to his second grade. I was at a little house party one day when I got a message that she had called. It was very odd that she would call me. I hadn't seen her in nearly a year. I stepped outside and called her back. She said, 'You need to get Michael out of that math class.' She was talking about her own class, remember. When I asked her why, she said, 'I have the Special Ed math class, the students with the lowest scores of all. Michael does not belong in that class.' At this point I didn't know he was even in that class!"

"Was she doing this on the sly?" I asked.

"Yes. She called me from her home so no one would know she was doing it. It was like something out of a spy novel. She said, 'He is becoming a different child. It's happening right before my eyes, and you don't want that to happen. You *can't* let it happen. You need to get him out of that math class. He's in with kids who are far below his level. You can't let his self-esteem suffer.' I already knew it was my number-one job to keep his self-esteem high. That was difficult because I could see that he was miserable in school. Up until then, I couldn't figure out why. When he started second grade, he had a complete personality change. He cried every night at the dinner table, and that just wasn't him. I would ask him what was wrong, but he would never tell me. So I was already worried and wondering what was going on, and then I got this call. I had recently found out about the little room where he was thrown in with a group for reading but not learning a thing. I had already tried to deal with that, but without much success."

"What happened?" I asked.

"I had heard the Special Ed teacher was leaving the school. She was the one who was in charge of that reading group, so I tried to make an appointment with her to talk about all of this. I tried for a month. Finally, on the day she was leaving, I got a chance to meet with her, and in that meeting all I did was cry. I couldn't talk at all. I couldn't ask a single question. I was just so frustrated by the whole thing. I felt that so much damage had been done to Michael because he was in that special room off the library. I felt it was really harming him. He would come home and say, 'Do I have special needs? Is there something wrong with me, Mom? Am I dumb?' It was horrible, and all I could do about it was cry!

"But that phone call rallied me. I decided I couldn't just cry about it. I had to *do* something. I had to take action. The day after the phone call telling me about the math class, I went down to the school to find out what was going on. I sent an e-mail first to set up a meeting."

"Was your e-mail answered?"

"No. Many of my e-mails were never answered, but I keep copies of them. I save everything. I have everything in writing. Every time I talk to someone, I follow it up in writing."

"And the teacher who didn't really know him—is she still in the picture?"

"Yes. She was still his teacher, so I included her in all the meetings."

"But she didn't know what was going on?"

"No. She didn't have a clue. As far as she was concerned, everything was great. Michael was still in the reading group and the math class, and I wanted him out of both of them. I wanted him back in the regular math class, and I wanted him to receive individualized reading instruction. I got nowhere with her in a one-on-one meeting, but by now, I was a little more educated than I was when I spent the meeting with the Special Ed teacher crying. I had read all the books, so I knew what I had to do. I had to call for a conference and explain my position. At the same time, I didn't want to be a pain in the neck. I knew I needed to keep them on my side. There is a balance you have to strike within the school. I have some other friends who don't seem to be getting anywhere, and I know the reason why. They're always filing complaints—which, admittedly, is part of the system. You have the right to do that. If you don't like the IEP, you have to reject it and file a complaint. The trouble is, the entire process seems designed to be as difficult and inefficient as possible. If you don't agree, you feel like you need to reject it outright because that's the policy. But when you do that, it then goes higher up to the state's Department of Education and you have to have a hearing and it takes all year to make what could sometimes be a simple point."

I agreed. "And apart from that, a confrontational attitude isn't always the best way to get things done," I said.

"That's right," Helen said. "Confrontation might seem satisfying because you have won and made your point, but at what cost? It can cause more problems than it's worth. It's best to try an unofficial, alternative approach first, rather than going immediately into an official dispute. If you have to file a dispute down the road, that's fine—but it shouldn't be the first course of action. When I had a problem, I would call the school and talk to them in a reasonable way. It's important that you act in a reasonable way. At the same time you also have to let them know that you know the system, and that you know what they are supposed to be doing. In many cases, they count on our ignorance and, because of that, some children slip through the cracks."

"Have you ever had a hearing?"

"No, I haven't. I thought we were headed that way during the time I wanted him out of those two classrooms. I think the only reason we didn't have a hearing was because I was so well prepared, with all my notes in a binder. Every time I sent a letter or e-mail, I cc'd the principal, the Special Education director, all the other Special Ed teachers, and the superintendent of the school. I kept a copy of every one of those cc'd letters and e-mails. I'm also on a committee with the superintendent, so I had some direct contact. You, as a mother, *must* become involved. It's critical. You can't just sit at home or at work and assume the best. You have to let the school know that you know what you're doing. You should have seen the conference meeting. Usually you go in the meeting with a Special Ed person and a teacher, but for this meeting, everyone was there. There were twelve people in the room. I had my son's doctor come in, too."

"That's a good idea."

"They act like you can't invite anyone, but this is not true. In fact, after I invited the superintendent, I called his secretary because they hadn't put his name on the list of people who were coming. They didn't put the doctor's name on, either. I pointed this out, and she said in an indignant way, 'Well! You can invite whoever you want,' as if I was somehow in the wrong or unreasonable for even thinking of doing such a thing. I said, 'Well, I did invite the doctor and he's coming, so you might as well put him on the list.' She said she wouldn't officially put him on the list because the school didn't want to pay his bill. I knew that I could invite whoever I wanted to the meeting because I looked it up.

"That is another point I would like to make to the mother new to all of this: you must arm yourself with knowledge. You need to know your rights and what you are entitled to. This secretary then said to me, 'It's not proper protocol to invite the superintendent.' And I said, 'You just said I could invite whoever I wanted.' I knew the superintendent wouldn't come, but I wanted to invite him anyway, just to make a point."

"What did you say at the meeting?"

"I said, 'Look, my son's not getting what he needs. He's so much worse off than he was before. I want him out of the math class and out of that reading group, too. I want him to get individual attention.' I also had an independent evaluation report with me. I had gotten so frustrated with the school system that a couple of months earlier, I had him evaluated on my own. I also had Michael's report card, which showed he got a B in reading. There's no way he could have gotten a B—he couldn't read! At the time I received the report card, I said to the head teacher, 'Is this serious? I don't want you to flunk my child, but this doesn't reflect the reality of the situation at all.' I wondered if they were just pushing him through. Later at that same meeting, I pulled out the report card and said, 'This is not acceptable. Giving him a grade like this is not helping him at all.'"

"This was the teacher who didn't really know him."

"Right," Helen said.

"What did she say when you pointed this out?"

"She kept saying in a condescending tone, 'You're doing the right thing. You have to be the advocate.' That sounds good, but she didn't mean it. It was her standard line. It was meant to pacify us and shut us up. My husband was at the meeting, too, and he was just so irritated by her. I had all I could do to control myself."

"Because you knew she wasn't paying attention to Michael?"

"Yes! She didn't mean any of it. You could tell it was just a set of words that didn't mean anything. She didn't know anything about him, but she gave him a B. He was also getting 100 on his spelling tests. He was spelling everything right, so on the surface, it may have seemed right to give him a 100. But you didn't have to go too far below the surface to see that he had absolutely no idea how to spell! I knew that because I would quiz him myself, and he would write down a word before I even said it. He had memorized the whole list of words and memorized the sequence of the letters. He couldn't spell, but he could certainly memorize. The doctor told me that the letters were more like symbols or pictures to him. They weren't letters. They weren't components of a word. He memorized them, but didn't understand them as language."

"The memorization showed his intelligence and ability to organize information."

"Absolutely. It's quite amazing, actually. I could never do it. But even so, he couldn't spell and he couldn't read. I could actually understand their rationale for wanting to put him in a special class for reading, but what I couldn't understand was why they took him out of his math class and put him into a special class far below his abilities. As far as I was concerned, he was a whiz at math. The teacher who called me told me he did the math assignment in the first few minutes and then he would sit there for the rest of the class drawing pictures of the *Titanic*. He came home with stacks of drawings of the *Titanic*. That's all he did in that class. He was completely bored, so he would tune everything out."

"Were you able to get him out of those classes?"

"Yes. Eventually we got everything we asked for. But the entire process was so confusing."

"Do you feel that it's *deliberately* confusing? Or just confusing?"

"A little bit of both. I think some schools rely on your ignorance. You have to educate yourself."

"Let's imagine a mother in the situation you faced," I said, "a mother just now starting off with the challenges of facing the school system. What advice would you offer?"

"First, if I felt that this mother was in any sort of denial, I would talk about the importance of getting help for her child. The next thing I would say is to buy a binder and keep everything in it—*everything!*—

and organize it by date. Keep every e-mail, every letter, a record of every conversation. If you have to go to a hearing down the road, those documents will be very helpful."

"What was the most helpful thing you did at this time?"

"Two things were extremely helpful. The first was getting an outside evaluation for my son, and the second was realizing I needed to create a paper trail by keeping copies of everything."

"Did you ever consider hiring an advocate?"

"I never got to that point, but if I couldn't figure all this out, I wouldn't hesitate to get an advocate."

How sad that any mother has to go through an ordeal similar to Helen's in order to get basic help for her child. Bureaucracies are put in place to help people, but often they become layered with so many regulations and protocols that they become unwieldy and lose sight of the very people they were meant to help. It's difficult enough raising a child with a disability, but the work and torment you sometimes have to go through to get that child the required help can seem totally unreasonable. Many schools are sympathetic to the plight of the mother—we mustn't lose sight of that—but some schools are not.

But take heart. Learn what you can. Keep records. Try to stay calm in the face of adversity. Keep your child's needs foremost in your mind, even if others do not. And know, always, that there are others out there who have gone through this before you. Find them and support one another.

In the next chapter we will explore the advocate option that Helen mentioned.

Chapter 16
Advocacy:
Advice from an Expert

Candace Cortiella, introduced in an earlier chapter, is the director of the Advocacy Institute, a nonprofit organization that develops projects, products, and services aimed at improving outcomes for children with disabilities—not just learning disabilities, but all disabilities. One of the institute's core activities is training Special Education advocates who work on behalf of parents and families. Candace is also the author of the *IDEA Parent Guide* so often cited in previous chapters, and I can think of no better person to talk to about the world of Special Education advocacy and the benefits and drawbacks of obtaining the services of an advocate for your child.

I began by asking what propelled Candace into the role of advocate.

"It is totally due to my daughter," she said. "My passion and devotion to advocacy can be traced back to having a young one who, at preschool age, was showing signs of developmental delay and a 'lack of school readiness,' as they called it in those days. That set into motion a series of extremely traumatic events that took me and my entire family down a long and difficult road."

"Essentially you were once one of the mothers we are trying to reach with this book," I said. "And I assume you remember all the confusion and the fear and the panic these mothers feel."

"Yes, and the sorrow."

"You have knowledge and experience from the point of view of both a mother and an advocate. Let's say you have just met a mother who is in the situation you were back when your child was in school. How would that mother find an advocate?"

"First, I would like to point out that a lot of mothers who think they need an advocate don't necessarily need one. Getting an advocate is not a decision that should be made lightly because injecting an advocate into a situation has both positive and negative consequences."

HIRING AN ADVOCATE

"What most often influences parents to make the very serious decision to hire an advocate?" I asked.

"Usually, it's when they feel that things aren't going right and that they don't have the capacity to get things done—whether it's knowledge, information, or the time and energy to deal with it themselves and move things along toward the results they're looking for. In some cases, advocates can very much stay in the background, and the parents can continue to play the role of facilitator with regard to whatever they are trying to accomplish. In other situations, advocates play a more direct role and accompany the parents to meetings and partake in sessions with private providers, school officials, and evaluators to become another set of eyes and ears."

"Let's look at both of those scenarios separately," I said. "Let's say a mother feels overwhelmed by the situation with her child. She's received the evaluation results and simply cannot understand what it all means. Would it then be possible to hire an advocate who could help her without the school knowing?"

"Yes, and often that is the best way to handle things. But if we go with the example you used of the mother not being able to understand the results of an evaluation, it is important to let parents know that schools have an obligation to provide parents with information that they can understand. It's very appropriate for a parent to say to a school, 'I need an opportunity to have an interpretive meeting about this evaluation before we go further in this process.' I was fortunate in that my daughter attended a school district that was rather large and sophisticated, and that practice was routine. They wanted parents to understand the evaluation results.

"So, first of all, parents should understand that they have the right to ask for interpretations of test results in understandable terms. Secondly, there is a whole system of Parent Training and Information Centers around the country to help parents. These PTI centers are funded by the federal government with IDEA dollars. Their mission is to help parents understand this whole morass of Special Education. So there are ways parents can seek that kind of help before they get to the point where they would need an advocate. But let's say they need to find an advocate. In some cases advocates are available through the PTI centers, or through a disability-specific organization or association—so there is a way to get an advocate without any cost. But in a lot of cases, advocates have to charge because this is how they make their living. But I hate to see parents pay for something when there are free alternatives."

"How much might an advocate charge?"

"I really can't say because there is such a vast range. There are people who try to keep their fees very low, and then there are people who work as advocates who also happen to be attorneys or well-trained educational diagnosticians. They bring a set of skills to the table, and they're going to charge more. As trainers of advocates, we have always encouraged them to do some pro bono work through the course of a year."

"If a family simply does not have the money for an advocate, can't they also approach their local Legal Aid Society?"

"That's right," Candace said. "There are also many Education Law centers around the country that work on all kinds of issues related to the education of children from low-income and minority families. They very often will have a Special Education component to them."

"So if a mother feels overwhelmed, she may want an advocate. But it sounds like you are strongly suggesting that she try to do as much as she can before taking that step."

"Absolutely."

"What is the best way to do that?" I asked. "How can a mother best educate herself about these issues?"

"The first thing to do is to take advantage of this network of Parent Training and Information Centers that I mentioned earlier. Educating parents about these issues is their purpose and their mission. There is at least one in every state, and some of the larger states have several. There are about a hundred all together. That is the first step parents should take. One of the reasons the PTI centers are so helpful is because, even though there is this federal law that governs Special Education, every state has its own particular policies and procedures put together in order to implement its Special Education obligations. This overlay of policies and procedures varies from state to state. For instance, I can learn about Special Education in Virginia and then move to California and all the terms are going to be different and there will be differences in the various policies. The training centers in each particular state have an expertise in that overlay."

A state-by-state listing of these centers can be found at www.ld.org/aspecialmother.

"You said there were both positive and negative aspects of having an advocate," I said. "The positive ones are pretty clear. This is someone who can guide you through the process. You can have this done without the school's knowledge, or without the advocate going to the school."

"That's right," Candace said. "If parents want to hire an advocate in more of a consulting role, then there would certainly be no reason for them to have to divulge to the school that they are working with an advocate."

"What is the downside of divulging to the school?" I asked. "And is this one of the negative aspects of hiring an advocate?"

"Sometimes, yes. Unfortunately, some schools consider parents bringing an advocate in to their case as a display of animosity. They can change their attitude and become quite defensive about the whole thing, which is a shame because, in a lot of cases, the advocate can be very helpful to the school as well as the parents. For example, when I was a practicing Special Ed advocate, it wasn't unusual for me to tell parents that their expectations were too high for what they were asking the school to do. Schools have an obligation, but those obligations also have parameters. Some parents think that the sky is the limit when it comes to the obligations of the school, and that is not the case. Sometimes the parents were more prepared to accept that from me than they were from the school."

"Sometimes a parent can become quite bitter and angry over the perceived treatment by the school," I said. "By no means am I saying they don't have legitimate concerns, but somewhere along the line the process broke down and was replaced by a completely antagonistic relationship. One mother I heard about filed so many disputes that everything was tied up for years, and the problems were kicked down the road a ways, but didn't go away. Eventually the school would not deal with her anymore, and she had to hire an advocate."

"There are times when that happens," Candace said. "For parents in those cases, winning their point becomes more important than what is best for the child."

"Some parents can become mired in these negative feelings," I added. "Something starts it—probably an issue that they feel the school didn't handle well. And maybe the school didn't handle it well, but then they begin to believe the school is handling *nothing* well, or that it is actively out to deny their child the services needed. There's no question that dealing with the school system can be a frustrating experience at times, but to fall into this quagmire of anger and resentment can do more damage than good. Do you run into this type of situation?"

"Yes, I do," Candace said. "And, of course, if you have a parent who also happens to be a professional of some kind, such as an attorney, that can present its own set of problems. They start becoming their own client in an area of law they don't know, and that can be difficult."

"One of our Special Mothers is an attorney, but she used her position in a positive way. She simply wrote her letters on her legal letterhead, and that seemed to get things moving. But in the cases we discussed, when all communication has broken down, can an advocate help the situation?"

"Sometimes, but certainly not always. We have had situations when we have had to essentially sever our working relationship with some parents. They won't listen, or follow our guidance. We have to say, 'We can't work with you. Your demands are unfounded. The manner in which you conduct yourself with the school people is doing nothing but deteriorating the relationship. It's doing nothing to benefit your child, and so you need to find someone else.'"

"What happens in that situation?" I asked. "What happens to that child? Do they just linger there without help?"

"Sometimes they do, yes. Sometimes parents take their kids out of the school and put them somewhere else, and then they continue to fight their battle. But in a lot of cases, the kids stay in whatever situation the parent is objecting to. So if they argue about it for two years, then the child is still there and not getting what the parents are arguing for. In cases like that, all the parents are doing is embittering themselves to the school district to the point where the school simply won't speak to them."

"What are some of the most common challenges parents face?"

"The thing that motivates parents to go to an advocate is essentially this: they are not getting whatever it is they want. There is no set pattern to the things parents want. In other words, it is difficult to pinpoint a single issue that is considered the greatest challenge. A lot of times parents want a more inclusive approach to the programming. I'm not talking only about LD here, but all disabilities. I think that is probably one of the most common issues for parents. They don't want the segregated placement that schools give them. They want something that is more inclusive."

"And what would you say is the most difficult to solve?"

"Again, the issue of inclusion is probably the most difficult," Candace said. "In most cases, if that is the issue, then the reason it is an issue is because the school or the district has always taken the segregated approach to children with disabilities. Therefore, getting what you want involves systemic change in the district. In fact, the most rewarding part of my work as an advocate over the years is when you help change something not only for one child but for a whole group of children. So systemic advocacy efforts are really at the heart of our work because we want things to be made better for all children. If we have six million children in Special Education in this country and we change it one child at a time, we're never going to live long enough to help them all. If we can improve the school experience of all children with disabilities, then we have made huge changes."

"What is the success rate for a parent who wants a more inclusive environment for her child?" I asked.

Candace hesitated. "That's a little difficult to answer," she said.

"Does it vary by school district?"

"Yes. Some simply refuse to do it."

"Does a parent have any recourse in that case?"

"The recourse is the Procedural Safeguards that are embedded in IDEA. This is also the level where you file a due process complaint, and that is not something to take lightly. This level of action is also the only one for which we have data, and that data shows that parents do not usually prevail. Most often the school prevails. So again, good advocates generally will not be the ones who are most eager to file due process. Rather, they try to solve the conflict at a much lower, informal level. That is why I had a hard time answering your question about the rate of success. We don't have data on how frequently disputes are settled at an informal level, nor do we have any real data on how successful those settlements might be."

GETTING A LAWYER INVOLVED

"I spoke to one mother who disagreed with something on her child's IEP and was told that she was perfectly free to dispute the issue, but it could take up to a year to solve the problem," I said. "She looked at her options and decided she didn't want to spend a year on what should have been a simple thing, so she was able to settle it informally. Is it true that something like a dispute can take up to a year or longer?"

"It shouldn't, but it can. And again, at the Advocacy Institute the person we would consider to be an effective advocate is not someone who beats the drum for parents to file a dispute right away. Filing a dispute puts your relationship with the school at a whole different level. The state gets involved. There is a timeline that starts ticking. This is a quasi-legal procedure, which is not to be taken lightly. And I have to tell you, a lot of parents will tell you with good reason that they are concerned that if they go to that level, the school may retaliate in some way, including possibly against their child. Just imagine it: you are having a quasi-legal process going on about your child, and at the same time you send the child there every day to interact with the same people you're in a dispute with."

"Why would someone go through all that?" I asked.

"What has become in vogue lately, mostly because of a major Supreme Court win, is that you take your child out of the public school and put the child in a private school, and then you sue the public school for tuition reimbursement. Those private school settings can be $30,000 to $40,000 a year. The parent can go back to the public school and say, 'You denied my child an appropriate education, which they are now getting in this private setting, therefore you must reimburse me.' But the attorneys who have a reputation for taking and winning those kinds of cases will usually say, 'All right, we'll get started on this as soon as you take your kid out of the public school.' As they develop their case, they don't want to have to be concerned with retribution against the child."

"Is it common for a parent to win in such cases?"

"Despite a couple of Supreme Court decisions finding in favor of parents in tuition reimbursement cases—*Forest Grove School District v. T.A.*, 2009, and *Florence County School District Four v. Shannon Carter*, 1993—these cases take many years and lots of resources to win. Fortunately, these favorable decisions serve as reminders to schools to make every effort to provide a program that delivers results for the student. Parents, in turn, should try to work with schools to develop a program that provides adequate progress."

WHEN THE SCHOOL SAYS NO TO SERVICES

I asked Candace if it is common (in her experience) for a school to reject services a parent feels the child needs.

"Oh, yes!" she exclaimed. "All the time."

"If that happens, what is the sequence of actions a parent should take?"

"It is a little dangerous to suggest that there is one pattern, because it is so dependent on the circumstances and on the size and complexity of what the parent is asking for. When we deal with parents around these issues, we have to be very careful, because an issue that seems enormous to a parent can seem rather trivial from my perspective as an advocate. The significance of what they want and are not getting is all in the eye of the beholder. For instance, a parent may want a full-time one-on-one aide, which can be a big issue for everybody involved. For the school it's a huge expense, and they may feel—with good reason, by the way—that they can address the child's needs without plastering an individual to them all day long. There is no specific set of services that are prescribed by the law. The law says only that you must provide the child with a free, appropriate public education, and that can leave a lot of room for the school to maneuver."

"That is an important point," I said. "It puts the school on a pretty strong footing. So let's say that a mother has heard that a certain type of service is effective for one child, and decides that is the type of service her own child should get—but the school, with legitimate reason, believes otherwise. They believe there is a way to do the same thing with less expense. The school's job is then to convince the mother that its method is equally successful, and the mother's job is to try to keep an open mind about this. She shouldn't just dig in her heels and say, 'No, I want this.'"

"That's right," Candace said.

"That will be tough for some parents to hear, especially if they feel the school hasn't been upfront with them on other issues. It's hard for them to accept that the school is telling the truth."

"That's true. And also, for that mother, it becomes an issue of saying, 'Okay, if I don't get this for my child, what will be the variance in how my child progresses?'"

"What do you mean?" I asked.

"Parents can easily get caught up in the details and lose sight of the big picture. At the end of the day, the important thing for parents is the progress made by the child, not whether or not that progress is made with whatever type of service the parent originally asked for. So if the school can give you the same progress, and it is appropriate and adequate for seventy-five cents as opposed to a dollar, then the parent really doesn't have much of a position on which to argue the need for the more expensive service."

"If a mother in that circumstance brought this to a dispute and the child's progress with the less expensive service was proven, would the parent lose?"

"Absolutely."

"So if a parent is insisting on something and the school is insisting on another thing that is as effective but less expensive, maybe that is the time to consult an advocate—even if it is only on this one issue. You don't need to bring the advocate into the school. It could be just a matter of asking the advocate's opinion to ease the parent's mind on whether or not the school is telling the truth and providing an equally valid service."

"Yes. That would absolutely be appropriate."

"I believe it comes down to a matter of trust in many cases," I said. "Some mothers simply do not believe what the school is telling them because they know that the school has a financial incentive to avoid providing certain services. For these mothers, it can be extremely difficult to get beyond that and accept that the school truly is doing something for the child's benefit as opposed to the school's benefit."

"That's true. And the fact is, public schools are always operating within the constraints of their finances."

"One of our Special Mothers, Helen, was never told that she had to officially ask to have her child evaluated. She was operating under the assumption that the school would step forward and tell her what she needed to do. From that point on, she couldn't shake the feeling that the school was not going to tell her things that were in the best interests of her child."

"The situation you just described goes further than the school simply neglecting to tell her," Candace said. "That school was actually violating their obligations under IDEA. Public schools have an *affirmative obligation* to identify and serve children with disabilities. It is not simply a matter of whether or not the parent asks. It goes much further than that. Denial of services and lack of responsiveness to parental concern is a very significant issue for schools. In fact, it is at the heart of that Supreme Court decision I mentioned earlier, *Forest Grove v. T.A.*, which was decided only in June 2009. The school district lost because it failed to be responsive to the parents' concerns and failed to identify and serve the youngster. It was a tuition reimbursement case, but the court's decision was very much driven by the fact that the school was callous and completely disregarded the concerns of the parents. And I'll tell you something, this Supreme Court decision has sent chills up the backs of every school district in this country!"

"This mother I mentioned faced a great deal of conflict and had to educate herself about the issues."

"She probably had to educate the school district, too. This is an important point. Parents should not presume that the schools always know fully and with thorough understanding what their obligations are, in terms of Special Education. The truth is that they don't always know."

"This notion might influence the way a parent approaches the school," I said. "For instance, when we talk about conflict resolution, rather than going into the school and throwing accusations around, it might be a good idea to start off by saying, 'Are you aware that you have this or that obligation?' In spite of all the horror stories we hear, we must emphasize that schools are not the enemy. Many teachers really do step forward and try to do the best they can."

"That is absolutely true," Candace said. "An informed parent can certainly be of help to both the school and the student. And again, the best way to become an informed parent is to take advantage of the resources provided by the Parent Training and Information Centers because they are federally funded and free to parents. That's what they are there for. The PTI centers will talk to you about the whole legal framework. To get disability-specific information, parents also need to rely on organizations such as the National Center for Learning Disabilities. You can find so much information online."

"There is a wealth of information out there," I said. "Parents have only to go to their computer to access it."

In that light, I would also like to mention the work of Pamela and Peter Wright, founders of the Wrightslaw Web site (www.wrights-law.com). For years, whenever a legal question came up from one of the thousands of mothers who called NCLD, we always directed them to the Wrights. They are experts in the field of Special Education law and have written several books. Many mothers have found their book *From Emotions to Advocacy* to be particularly helpful.

For more about the work of the Advocacy Institute and advocacy in general, please visit their Web site at www.advocacyinstitute.org.

Chapter 17
Resolving Disputes

Let's face it: sometimes the system breaks down. Communication becomes tense and unproductive. Someone refuses to listen to someone else, and soon the tension escalates into something approaching all-out war. Before we get to the issue of resolving disputes, let's talk a little about how and why disputes arise. I'm going to come at this in two ways: first, when the parent is being unreasonable and aggressive (not *you*, of course!), and second, when the difficulty comes from the school.

When talking about an unreasonable parent, it is not so much a matter of dispute resolution as it is dispute avoidance. There's no point in pretending that every mother in the United States wears a halo and all problems that arise with the school are the fault of the mean, vicious teachers and principal. If someone is already a little fragile and prone to martyrdom, it will not take long for this person to believe the school is out to get her, or is purposely doing harm (for now, let's leave out the possibility that the school really *is* out to get her). It is also not unusual to find a mother who is by nature level-headed and rational, but who is so shaken by the bureaucracy that she can become someone whose anger and sense of victimhood surprises even her. I will touch on some of this in the final chapter, which explores ways to get yourself out of this predicament. For now, let's talk about how you might get there in the first place, and ways to avoid it.

It often comes down to a matter of trust. Let's take the example of Helen, who found out by chance that she could have her son tested only if she forthrightly asked for it. Once she did ask the school, he was scheduled for a test. But that problem planted a little seed in Helen's mind. It could have stayed a seed and eventually been forgotten, but the road to Special Education is lined with opportunities to water that seed and allow it to grow into a tree of suspicion and doubt. It soon reached a point where Helen began to doubt everything they told her, and could not shake the feeling that they were not doing all they could for her son.

This is so common. We all know that public schools are constrained by budgetary considerations. We would like to believe that they would happily toss those considerations aside for the sake of a child with special needs, but we know better. Of course, you can always find wonderful teachers who are more than willing to help, or well-funded school districts that offer the best services available; but too many parents find themselves in a situation where they suspect— no, they *know*—that the school is not being straight with their answers or offers of support.

This issue must be dealt with in ways that do not send you off the deep end. I have met mothers and fathers so consumed with angst and fury at both real and imagined injustice by the school system that they render themselves incapable of mounting an effective offense. They arrive at the school and storm down the hall armed with accusations and insults, alienating everyone, including those who might otherwise have been allies. Their home lives suffer, too. They can talk of nothing else. Their spouses are ready to jump out a window, that's how sick to death they are of hearing, yet again, how the school is cheating their child. Marriages can falter, and sometimes end. Friends fall by the wayside, no longer willing to listen to the broken record of complaint. Sometimes an advocate must be called in because the school flatly refuses to have any further direct dealings with that parent. Worst of all, the child suffers, both at home and at school.

Often this type of parent files dispute after dispute, which may in the end settle the issue but may also be too late. While a dispute is ongoing, the chances are the child is not receiving the services the parent desires. People—not just teachers, but *all* people—are fallible human beings. Some may take secret pleasure in thwarting your wishes, just for the satisfaction of denying you what you want. You attack. They defend. Your chances are infinitely better if you are able to step back, take a deep breath, and attempt to approach things in a rational, reasonable way.

Note that I said *attempt*. Some simply cannot do it, or the conflict has escalated beyond any hope of repair through rational discussion.

The best defense against this type of tortured relationship with the school is to do all you can to avoid it in the first place. This may take a mighty effort on your part, especially if you are sure of the rightness of your cause. Do not lose sight of that cause, which is the well-being and education of your child. As Candace warned in the previous chapter, *do not let winning your point become the cause*. It's quite possible to win your point and stand back with a satisfied smile, only to discover you have left a trail of wreckage behind that has done little to help your child and may, in fact, have made the problems worse.

YOU AND YOUR CHILD'S SCHOOL

So how should you deal with the school?

Here are a few simple suggestions that could help smooth the way, or at least prevent a shouting match.

When you go to the school for a meeting with a teacher, get there on time. Trying to find a parking spot, then racing down the hall to your appointment that started ten minutes earlier, is a sure way to make yourself frazzled and anxious, and the teacher irritated.

Dress for success. I've mentioned this before. Don't show up for a school meeting in your gym shorts. These are serious issues. Appear as if you take them seriously.

Be open-minded and listen. Do not barge in with a list of complaints and rattle them off without giving the other party a chance to respond. In the same vein, do not go in believing you know exactly what they'll say, and therefore you don't really need to hear it. We can all conjure up conversations in our minds before they happen, but the truth is, we don't know what they will say. If you listen and give them a chance to actually say what they want to say, not what you *think* they'll say, you may be surprised.

Bring notes and take notes. Arrive at the meeting with a written list of questions and/or concerns. You don't want to leave the building and say, "Oh darn, I forgot about this," and race back in for an unscheduled follow-up. At the same time, you don't want to rely only on your memory to remember what is said in the meeting. Jot things down, and keep those notes in your Master file. If necessary, ask to have a follow-up meeting that you will attend in exactly the same mature, responsible way.

These suggestions could help, but sometimes the situation cannot be diffused through good communication and interpersonal skills. Sometimes there is a genuine disagreement. Let's say you disagree with the IEP, for example.

The first thing you must do is notify the IEP team of your disagreement. You can do this by phone. Whether or not the disagreement is settled immediately, you should always follow up with a letter that describes your phone conversation and details exactly what you want changed. Things will often be settled at this level through a meeting to work out the details or, at least, written documentation of what will be changed. But if the IEP team is not able to resolve the problem, you then move on to the Special Education director for your school district. You explain the problem, and that you tried unsuccessfully to resolve it with the IEP team. Again, specify the problem and your proposed solution, and once again follow up with a letter detailing the conversation. There's no guarantee that you will get what you want, but if you feel strongly about the issue, keep trying. Keep things at the local level as long as possible. Don't stop with only one phone call or letter. Call several times. Really make an effort to get them to pay attention. If they don't, or if they refuse or fail to change the IEP, move on to the next level.

Situations may arise through negligence or stubborn opposition on the school's part that simply cannot be reconciled through phone calls and meetings. If a parent strenuously objects to a school district's assessment or educational programs for their child, or believes the school district has violated any of the requirements of IDEA, that parent may have no choice but to file a dispute.

As Candace Cortiella noted in the previous chapter, this is not something a parent should take lightly. By filing a dispute you have fundamentally changed the dynamic of the parent-school relationship. Even so, there are times when that's exactly what a parent wants and needs to do.

LEVELS OF DISPUTE

Luckily, a dispute does not automatically mean a trip to the courthouse. There are levels of dispute resolution. Entire books have been written about this subject, so I will cover them briefly here. For further information on dispute resolution, visit www.wrightslaw.com.

Mediation

Mediation is a voluntary process of negotiation between parents and the school. It brings in a trained, impartial mediator who helps resolve the disagreement without a formal due process hearing. This is the least formal (and in many ways most preferable) method to resolve a dispute.

Due Process Complaint (Request for Hearing)

This is a written complaint to request a hearing involving any matter related to the identification, evaluation, or educational placement of the child or the provision of a free appropriate public education. Either the parent or the school district may request the hearing, which is conducted by the state's Department of Education or by the local school district.

To file the due process complaint, you must provide the school district (or its attorney) and your state Department of Education with a written notice that includes the name and address of the student, a full description of the problem, and your proposal to solve the problem (if you have one). This written notice must include every issue that you would like addressed at the hearing. Unless the school district agrees, you will not be able to bring up additional issues you did not include in the initial complaint (though you may file a separate request for another hearing).

When the state Department of Education receives the written notice, it will assign a hearing officer to your case. Within five days, the hearing officer will review your case and determine whether your request meets IDEA's requirements for a due process hearing. You will be notified of the decision in writing.

The school district should also respond to your request with an explanation of why the district proposed or refused to take the action as noted in the request for a due process hearing. They will also describe other options considered by the IEP team, and a description of each evaluation procedure, assessment, record, or report that the school district used as the basis for the proposed or refused action. At this point, the parties can also agree to go to mediation rather than moving forward with the due process complaint.

Resolution Session

Within fifteen days of the time a parent filed a due process complaint, the school district must hold a meeting between the parents and the relevant members of the IEP team to discuss the complaint. This resolution session must include a representative from the school district who is authorized to make decisions on behalf of the school district.

Here are a few things you should know about the resolution session:

- If you do not bring an attorney to the meeting, the school district is not allowed to bring one, either.
- If an agreement is reached in this session, it is legally binding, though you have three business days after the meeting in which to void it if you wish.
- If the complaint is not resolved to your satisfaction within thirty days of the resolution session, the due process hearing may occur.
- If for some reason you refuse to participate in this meeting, the school district can request that the complaint be dismissed by the hearing officer.

Due Process Hearing

This is a formal, quasi-legal procedure before an impartial hearing officer or Administrative Law judge who is not an employee of the state Education Department or school district. Both the parents and the school personnel present arguments and evidence. If the hearing officer determines that the school district is at fault, you may be awarded reasonable attorney's fees. If, on the other hand, the hearing officer determines that your attorney has requested the hearing for reasons that are frivolous or unreasonable, that officer may award reasonable attorney's fees to the school district. The officer may also do this if he or she finds that a parent or the parent's attorney has requested a due process hearing for an improper purpose such as to harass, cause unnecessary delay, or needlessly increase the cost of litigation. Again: these hearings should not be undertaken lightly, or without legitimate reason.

Civil Lawsuit

This is the most extreme option. If parents are not satisfied with the results of the due process hearing, they may file a civil suit against the state or school district within ninety days of the hearing officer's decision in the due process hearing. They would have to hire an attorney and go through extensive legal proceedings. A lawsuit should be filed only if it is the only option that will resolve the dispute and ensure that the child receives appropriate services.

It is certainly to be hoped that any problems you have with your school can be resolved effectively without involving the courts. But they are there for a reason and sometimes they present the only choice.

As we know, conflicts do not take place only in the school. For some mothers, the greatest source of conflict occurs in the very last place they expect to find it: their own home. This can be the most painful of all, as we'll discover in the next chapter.

Chapter 18
Special Fathers: They Are Out There

Although there are exceptions, mothers and fathers tend to handle situations differently, and these differences are often exacerbated when learning disabilities appear on the horizon. This is not to say that some fathers do not play an equal, or even primary, role when dealing with a child with LD. And many more who are unable to play that primary role provide emotional and financial support to their wives. Having said that, I believe I would be doing a disservice not to acknowledge those mothers who cannot help but feel they have been unfairly burdened with the stresses and frustrations of dealing with the emotional toll that comes with raising a child with LD.

Some fathers simply sweep the issue under the rug and pretend it does not exist. For their wives, this lack of interest and support from their partner becomes the single most agonizing aspect of the challenge of LD. It outweighs all the frustrations caused by teachers and evaluators. It gnaws at them day and night: *Why can't he see this? Why won't he take the trouble to listen to my concerns? Two people are better than one, and I need him to help deal with the bureaucracy of the school system.*

Many women who adore their husbands and believe them to be wonderful and attentive fathers can still feel deprived of support when it comes to LD. What is it about the so-called hidden disabilities that makes it difficult for so many men to get involved? It can put a strain on the marriage. Husbands and wives who otherwise share similar outlooks and interests can suddenly find themselves diverging into two irreconcilable camps. One might be at the denial stage while the other has already accepted the situation. One might insist on an evaluation while the other balks due to fears of labeling. There are so many traps we can fall into, and so many times when we need to rely on our own gut feelings rather than a set of guidelines, that misunderstandings and miscommunication seem inevitable.

Though fathers may adore their children, LD does not always seem to be a priority for them, whereas it often becomes a *total* priority for mothers. Fathers will usually come around to some level of understanding and acceptance, but it can be a long road. They may believe their wives are exaggerating the problem, or even creating it. "As far as he's concerned," one mother told me, "he's got this crazy lady in bed beside him night after night, reading from a stack of fifty-seven books about learning disabilities, and he believes those books have given her ideas!"

I have spoken with far too many mothers who tell me their greatest challenge has been the attempt to get their husbands on board. In speaking with the Special Mothers Club, I noted that they all had some degree of frustration with their husbands' lack of involvement. Why is this?

DANA: "HE DOESN'T SEE THIS THE SAME WAY I DO"

"It seems to me that a lot of the dads have a harder time accepting things, especially with a son," Dana said. "They have a harder time recognizing it, or acknowledging it, or even understanding. Boys are boys, as far as they're concerned. That's what my husband thought. And this is the interesting thing: my husband had been home with the boys for years. He had the contact with the boys every single day, but he didn't see things the same way I did. He's a great dad; he's an amazing dad. But it's easier for him to say, 'My son is normal—there's nothing wrong,' and by saying that, it made me feel like he was saying, 'What is wrong with you? Why are you so dramatic?' And I'm not so dramatic. I'm really not.

"In talking about the father's role in all this," Dana continued, "I would like to first point out that many of us count on the father to be the tough-love parent figure, as they traditionally have been. My husband is much tougher with my sons, and they need that. That's my husband's perspective: things are tough sometimes and you've got to make do with them. I surely do not outright disagree with that opinion, so I get a little annoyed when my husband seems to imply that I think the world needs to be candy-coated for my boys. I think a lot of men think everything is a problem if you're a woman. Husbands think that mothers create these problems and that we overanalyze and we get overemotional and we get just plain old silly—and it irritates them. But they don't feel the same kind of gut feelings about their children. And let me tell you, my husband definitely has some gut feelings about his kids. There have been many times when I've been wrong and he's been right. But when it comes to this kind of thing, a disability, he just doesn't seem to feel it. My gut feelings have definitely led the way on this. My husband has fought it all along the way. At the same time, I count on him to help me step back and say, 'You know what? This part is normal. This is not a big deal.'"

"Have you come to some form of acceptance about this?" I asked.

"It depends on the day," Dana said with a laugh. "I am trying harder to be accepting of the fact that he doesn't see this the same way I do. That helps. At the same time, there is no denying that the only way he could really listen was when we were sitting at a table with five members of the school staff saying the same things I already said—that's the only way he could really listen."

"How did your husband come around?" I asked. "Or has he?"

"He has definitely come around, but he is still not the type of person who is going to call the school or e-mail the teacher to ask how things are going. But we always go to the conferences together—for all our kids, not just James. So he's not disengaged. In fact, he has by necessity taken a more active role in my son's issues. James sees a psychologist once a week. Whenever I took him, he was rebellious, rude, and utterly unable and unwilling to enter the room and engage in a conversation on any level. I couldn't figure out how to put a stop to this behavior so that we could actually make some progress, rather than spending our sessions dealing with James's attitude. My husband stepped in and began taking him, and it was instantly a different scenario. As a bonus, my husband now gets to hear for himself some of the things James has on his mind, the things my husband assumed I had 'fed' to James. It hasn't changed a thing about my being the primary advocate, but it helps—and I sure did need help.

"The whole situation didn't have to be as hard as it was. It was a billion times harder than it had to be because I had my husband saying 'You're overdramatizing; they don't know what they're talking about; look how dramatic you're getting.' And then, when he finally accepted it, the situation became, in my mind, 'He thinks I'm doing it wrong, and therefore he thinks I'm a bad mother.' Of course, he never *says* those things—but I end up thinking that. And it's very difficult because I think he is a great person. I really respect him and I really admire him, so battling against him is difficult because I care so much about what he thinks. It matters so much to me that we are a team. And to go into something like this without your partner is difficult. It's terrible to feel you're alone."

DEBORAH: "HE COULDN'T FIX IT"

At first Deborah's husband, Johnny, didn't understand the situation. "Back when I first suspected there might be a problem with our daughter Windy," she says, "I expressed my fears to Johnny."

"What did he say?" I asked.

"'Deborah, she's fine,' he would say."

"So you were alone for the most part."

"I was alone at the beginning of the journey. Most men, I suppose, hear about the problem, go right for the solution, want to fix it and move on. But in this situation, there was no quick solution. At this stage, I used this phrase about my husband: 'He could neither fix it nor face it.' I have since realized and accepted that that was part of his journey, but during the time that it was happening, it was a lonely road for me."

"When did that end?"

"Once Windy was professionally diagnosed, a wonderful woman, Flo Glasgow, who established Children's House as a center for children with difficulties, became my wise counselor and friend. She came along when I needed her most, and I don't know what I would have done without her. She spent time with me, and then she would talk to both Johnny and me about Windy and our family dynamics. In time, Johnny became more aware of Windy's full situation. That understanding can be pivotal in the journey. Johnny has a heart of gold. He has a huge heart, but he just didn't understand it all and he couldn't fix this one.

He didn't know what to do. And he will tell you now, if he sat down with us right now, he would say it took a long time for him."

"A lot of the mothers I talk to are right in the middle of this situation," I said. "Nearly all of them have an issue with their husband's not accepting their child's disability, and then they very quickly say, 'But he's a wonderful father.'"

"And that's true," Deborah said. "They are wonderful fathers, but they still have trouble accepting reality for what it is. I believe that we all do the best we can at the time with the information we have. Remember, that was thirty-five years ago and there wasn't a lot of information or resources out there. We were young and Windy was our first child, and it was hard. However, if I said, 'Johnny, we need to drive somewhere and have her tested, or to see this or that professional,' he would do it immediately and be glad to have some role to play. For Windy, her father was there for her. Just this morning she said, 'Oh, Mom, you were there for me, but so was Daddy. He was there, too.' In her mind, he was always there for her, and that is important to me."

I understand that, because Allegra feels that her father was always a part of her life, too. The reality is that her father was not a part of her life, and never had been. We divorced when Allegra was less than a year old, and he took no further role in her life. Even so, Allegra has created an ideal father in her mind—and I'm happy for that. He passed away a couple of years ago and she has only good memories.

JANIE: "HE DOESN'T LIKE THE BATTLE"

Janie's husband was on board from the beginning, but he still has trouble understanding LD. "He sometimes thinks it's a problem with my son's attitude," Janie says, "and I keep telling him that it's not attitude—it's a learning disability. But the reality is that LD sometimes can be so annoying. It takes so much energy just to live with it. And bedtime is a nightmare. It's like running your fingernails down a chalkboard. My husband and I are always like, 'Oh, no, we have to put him to bed…here we go.' Homework is even worse. Sometimes my son gets it, and then suddenly he doesn't. My husband gets very stressed about it. The first thing he says when he gets home is not, 'Hi, how are you?' It's 'Is the homework done?' And I get so irritated and think,

'If you dare say that one more time!' So he says, 'Is the homework done?' and I say, 'You want to start? Come on! Bring it on!'"

"So he comes home hoping it's done?" I asked.

"Yes! Because he doesn't like the battle. My kids are very active and very social. They have a lot of playdates, and my husband thinks the problem is because Marky has too many playdates. He thinks that's why he can't do his homework or has trouble reading, but I think that without the playdates, Marky doesn't have enough of an outlet. He has nothing to look forward to. I would give him playdates around the clock if that's what it took for him to feel connected and social. I would rather say to my kids, 'Let's forget the homework—go read an Easy Read book.' That to me is homework. In school, when they read, Mark looks like a model student. He's a good boy, but he has trouble reading. I say to my husband, at the end of day, 'Was he kind to other kids? Did he mouth off? Did he have to go to the principal's office? Are we having issues where we need to take him to a hospital? No, we're not. So he doesn't want to do the homework peacefully. So what?'

"But even that is changing. He has a little brother who is coming up after him, and Mark sees how smoothly it goes. You don't have to say to him a million and twenty times, 'If you just do it, and you just sit quietly, there is a reward at the end of it.' Because with the younger brother, no one is yelling, no one is being sent for time out. With Mark, it was always endless threats. My husband would say, 'That's it, there's no more Gameboy! That's the problem!' You see? My husband always tries to find 'the problem.' It's either playdates, or Gameboy, or something else when, truly, the problem is learning disabilities."

JOHN: A SPECIAL FATHER

I decided to get the other side of the story, and spoke with someone I know for certain is a Special Father. His name is John. His son Charlie, now enrolled in a program for college-aged students with learning disabilities, has some physical challenges that go beyond the confines of LD. Unlike most of us who find out our child has a disability a few years down the road, John knew there was a problem the day his son was born. Charlie was in the nursery and his hand was twitching. If it was only twitching, it would have stopped when the nurse touched it, but it didn't stop. They did a CAT scan and a pediatrician walked into the room where Charlie's mother was lying in a hospital bed (having gone through twenty-four hours of labor) and said to both parents, "Part of your son's brain is missing."

John's reaction was, understandably: "I could have shot the guy."

Charlie was helicoptered to Children's Hospital in Philadelphia, where they discovered he was born without a corpus callosum, the bundle of nerves that links the two hemispheres of the brain. It was a random genetic event that resulted in severe learning disabilities.

John has always been devoted to all his children, and with the birth of Charlie, he became deeply immersed in every aspect of his son's disability. He is not a stay-at-home father. He is a hard-working executive at a financial firm. His hours are long, but his dedication to all of his children is total.

I met with John in his Manhattan office to talk about Charlie and the role of the father in the life of a disabled child. We started by discussing the title of the book. "How do you feel about A *Special Mother?*"

"I think it makes sense," John said. "There are a lot of two-income families these days," he explained, "but whenever I took the day off to deal with an issue with Charlie's school, I was generally the only dad there. Even so, that doesn't mean that the father can't be Special. They have great influence over their children, those with LD and those without. I know a few guys who are very involved with learning disabilities, but a lot of them don't get involved."

"Why do you think that is?" I asked.

"I don't know," he said. "Maybe they think it's not their 'job,' it's not their 'problem,' and they've got enough other issues to deal with. I think some of it is denial—though I think denial can swing both ways, by the way. Some mothers can't or won't acknowledge the problem. And also, most of the parent-teacher meetings take place in the day, so you either have to work from home that day or take the day off. I'm sure there are a lot of dads who are not able to attend. If you're working on an assembly-line job, you're not taking an hour off. Of course, there are many mothers who work full-time jobs, too, but I still think society is more understanding of the mother taking the hour off to go to a school meeting than it is for the father. Fair or unfair, that seems to be the reality on the ground."

"Have your other children had any trouble with Charlie's disabilities?"

"Charlie has a brother, James, who is five years younger. When James was growing up, Charlie was walking and talking and taller, so James was looking at him as someone to emulate. As time passed, Charlie's progression continued to be slow and James progressed beyond him. I think of it as James going from looking at his brother through his developmental windshield to looking at him in the rearview mirror. And that has continued apace. Charlie will never drive a car, but James will be sixteen next summer and he'll want a car."

"Did you ever have to talk to James about Charlie?" I asked.

"When he got older, yes. And that's what I meant by the influence a father can have. The first time I spoke to him about it was when Charlie started playing in Special Olympics basketball. James came along to the event, and there were a large number of children there with Down syndrome. James looked at all these people who looked similar and asked if they were all brothers and sisters. I explained that it was a particular disability, and that it was an issue with their genes. I said, 'It's different than the one Charlie has, but he also has an issue with his genes. And that's why his motor skills aren't as good as yours, and his intellect is less than yours. It doesn't make him anything less than a wonderful human being, but his development has essentially come to a halt. So you are going to be doing things he will never be able to do, and be sure you don't ever give him any grief about it.' And he never has. He would never say something like, 'Ha-ha, I can ride a bike and you can't.' It would never occur to him to say something like that.

"He's very protective of Charlie. A lot of people are, because he's such a nice guy. And when you first look at Charlie, you don't look at him and think he's got a problem. If you look at his picture you don't say, 'There's a special needs kid.'"

"That is one of the most difficult things about LD," I said.

"You can't see it. And sometimes people expect more than these kids are capable of giving. With the invisible disorders, whether it's ADHD or dyslexia, you can't see it. Sometimes the school picks it up

and intervenes to solve the problem, but other times the school does-
n't pick it up at all and the teachers essentially say, 'All our other kids
are so bright; why is he so slow?' The ironic thing is that he could be
the brightest one of the bunch. But when he looks at the page, the
words are all upside down."

"A lot of parents are deathly afraid of the Special Ed label. Were
you ever afraid of Charlie being labeled?"

"No. I can only assume that people who are afraid of labels are
concerned that if they acknowledge that their child has a disability,
then people will think it's their fault."

"Some parents wait too long to get their child evaluated because
they're afraid of the labels."

"The problem with that is that they will have to get the child evaluated someday. Why wait? It's called Special Ed because these kids
need something special to progress. And if you are in denial and put
them in a regular classroom where they are fortieth out of forty all the
time, then you are doing terrible harm. And as I say, I can only assume
that the motives for doing this are more about oneself than about the
child. I hate to say it, but I think a lot of this denial is about the parent not wanting to acknowledge the problem, worrying more about
what people will say or that they will think the parent has done something wrong."

I then said, "That assumes that you think you're going to be able
to hide it forever."

"Right," John said. "But the problem is not going to go away. It's not
like your child's dyslexia will disappear when he turns fourteen. Happy
Birthday—you're not dyslexic anymore. Mothers *and* fathers need to
accept their situation for what it is, not for what they want it to be."

Bravo, John! I wish that every father could be as proactive and
committed as he is, but we all know that is not the case. Sometimes it
is best to sit back and let someone else talk to your husband. I know
of one mother in New York City who called the guidance counselor at
the school and asked her to help convince her husband of their child's
LD. She said, "You and I and the teacher know where we stand with
my daughter, but I can't find the words to make my husband listen. I
need the words. Will you help me?" The guidance counselor asked for
everyone to meet. She suggested that the woman tell her husband that

the school called the meeting. "To this day he has no idea that I called the meeting in order to make him hear it from somebody else," she told me. "We had to trick him. It pains me that I felt I had to do that, but he thought the teacher didn't know what she was talking about. So there I was, completely and utterly alone, without his support."

If you find yourself in a similar situation, here is some advice given directly to your child's father from another father.

Bookmark the page. Hand the book to your husband. Say, "Here. Read this," and see what happens.

It might help.

ADVICE TO A FATHER FROM A FATHER

Our Special Father, John, answered some questions posed by a young man who is having trouble dealing with the fact that his child has a disability. John prefaced his remarks by saying, "From my own experience, I can't understand why anyone would deny it. In my case, we knew about Charlie's disability on the day he was born, but if my other son had been tested in third grade and found to have LD, my first reaction would not have been to deny it. It would have been, 'What are we going to do to solve the problem?'"

Q: *Young Father: But I don't want my son to be labeled. I am afraid of the stigma.*

A: If there is going to be any stigma attached, it will not help to hide from reality. If you do, the stigma will come anyway. It will come because of the child's behavior. I don't have an issue with labels. My only issue is with people who would not do whatever it takes to bring their child as far along as possible. If the child isn't going to make it to the finish line as a typical adult, bring him as far through the race as you can. If they don't make it to the end, where they become a partner at Goldman Sachs, well, so what? My son Charlie would be very happy to spend the rest of his life as a clerk in the hardware store, and he will think he has achieved. And he has! If fathers think, "If all he does in life is to be a clerk, what am I going to say?" it won't help at all. Relative to what could have happened to him, Charlie has achieved. It's just on a different scale. You cannot judge how well your child is doing based on a peer group composed of children who don't have special needs or LD.

Q: *Young Father: I'm not sure I believe my child has LD at all.*

A: Again, you have to think first about the child before you think about yourself. Nobody's view matters so long as your child gets help. Learning disabilities are not a function of a failure on the part of either parent. Failure to deal with them *is*. You can't be blamed for the fact that your child has LD, but you can certainly be blamed for the fact that you didn't do anything about it. Denial is detrimental to the well-being of your offspring—and why would you do that? It doesn't make any sense.

Q: *Young Father: But I don't have time. I'm working too hard. I just can't deal with this.*

A: You have to *make* time. If you are working a job where you really are working many, many hours, and if you can't actively participate, then make sure you provide the emotional and moral support to the partner who is participating. If you can't give time, give encouragement. Give support. Do whatever you can to help facilitate the process.

Q: *Young Father: How can I do that?*

A: Be supportive. Be there emotionally. When you get home after a long day at work, *ask* your wife what happened that day. Ask if there is anything more that you can do. Give what you can. If you can't give time, give moral, emotional, and financial support. This can be expensive stuff.

Q: *Young Father: And what if I don't involve myself? My wife is handling it—she doesn't need me.*

A: If you can't give the support that's required, then frankly, my reaction would be: shame on you. That sounds tough, and it is. Shame on you. It's your child. Without you, there would be no child. If you helped bring that child into the world, you have to help bring that child along. It's your responsibility. And like I said, if you're working very hard or working two jobs, at some point just thank your wife for what she is doing.

Q: *Young Father: But I wanted my son to be a doctor or an investment banker. That was my dream, and now it's not going to happen.*

A: All right, so you know it's not going to happen. So your responsibility now is to help him be as much as he can be with the skills God gave him. Okay, so he wasn't dealt fifty-two cards. He got forty-seven cards. So help enable him to do something with what he was given. You should feel wonderful if all you are able to do is to get him through high school and into some occupation that suits his skill level. You should be very proud of having done that, rather than sitting around and moping about the fact that he's not going to be an investment banker—because he's not. Denial won't change that.

Q: *Young Father: What about the school meetings? My wife wants me to go. Should I?*

A: If you can, you should. School authorities think they can push the mothers around. I don't know why that is, whether it's still a male society or whatever; but I think they feel they can push the mothers around. If there is a united parental front, it makes them say, "Uh-oh, these guys are serious."

Q: *Young Father: What should I know before going to the meeting?*

A: Know your rights. Too many parents go to these meetings thinking they have to do only what they are told. That's so wrong. The school has to do what you tell them to do—it's your child. And they can schedule meetings early in the day or late in the day to try to accommodate your schedule. It doesn't have to be at noon. I commute, so I would ask them to make the meeting at four p.m. so I could leave work early that day. I think school districts respond better to two parents. If it's just a mother, they have one response. If it's just a dad, they have another. But if both of you are there, you are going to have a much better chance of getting what you want. School districts will try to do things that fulfill *their* needs, not the child's needs. They care about the children, but they also have a business to run. *You have to go in there assuming they're going to give you nothing.* So you have to know what is on the menu, and which things on there you want.

When I hear John say things like this, it saddens me. Schools should not be run as a business. Schools are a child's second home, a place where teachers fill in for the mother for a couple of hours each day and prepare our children for their future. They are also a place where friendships begin and, with any luck, flourish.

Chapter 19

Friendship Is So Hard: The Social Side of LD

Imagine these two situations.

First, your child comes home with another report card filled with Cs and Ds, evidence yet again that she has struggled to keep up in school and failed.

Second, you see your child off to the side in the schoolyard, all alone, watching others her age play a game you just *know* she desperately wants to join.

I'm sure you can well imagine which of these two situations most breaks a mother's heart.

Friends are our anchors, our support systems, our touchstones. They are what sweetens a childhood, and a lack of them can diminish childhood in ways that last well into adulthood.

When your child has no friends, when no phone calls from childish voices disrupt your dinner, when no one ever asks your son to stay overnight, or your daughter to join in a hopscotch game, all anxiety and sadness over poor reading scores or bad report cards pale by comparison. Nothing—*nothing*—tears at our emotions quite like this.

I remember it vividly, and I still clench my fists in anger and residual sadness when I think of the girls who should have been Allegra's friends falling by the wayside, one by one. It was especially difficult in the summer. We lived in a large community of children, all on summer break, all sharing toys, and houses, and the secrets all children share. The sound of giggling and laughter was absent in our house during these times. Friends were more important than anything else in

those long summer days, and I did my best to give Allegra every opportunity to have playdates. I had parties and cookouts at our house. I
made sure I had the latest gadgets and toys. I tried to make our house
the most fun of any in the neighborhood. But regardless of how many
times they came over, the children would all eventually come up with
excuses for why they couldn't come again.

This never stopped Allegra. When she makes up her mind to do
something, she has to do it. It would start in the morning: she would
get the idea that she wanted somebody to come over and play. She
would go to the phone and my heart would stop every time because I
already knew the answer: "No, I can't come over today. No, I'm too
busy. No, I'm going over to Ellie's house." She would try first one, and
then another, and then another, and again, "No, I can't come today.
No, I'm going over to So-and-so's house instead." After the first couple of calls I would try to change the morning around by suggesting we
go to town or go shopping—anything to distract her from the telephone. I often wonder why the parents of these young girls never
encouraged them to include Allegra, or made them aware that not
everyone is perfect and that you have to reach out sometimes and
make an effort to include others who are not exactly like you.

The invitations never came. The phone did not ring or, if it did,
the person at the other end was one of my son's friends asking him
over to play. Without the opportunity to play with kids her own age,
Allegra retreated into the behavior that would become one of the
hallmarks of her life: she would spend her time with older people,
mostly older women. I can honestly say that her best friend in those
summer days was Maria, the woman who used to cook for us.

I have often comforted myself over the passing years by the thought
that Allegra really didn't understand what was going on, or wasn't as
aware of her lack of friends as I was. But then I ran across an evaluation
report written when Allegra was twelve that proves she most certainly
did understand what was going on. She never said as much to me, but
(with her permission) here is what the evaluation contained:

Interpersonal relationships are extremely important to Allegra
and she has a powerful need for attachment to others. Her feel-

ings about her mother are strong and positive, and she is emotionally very dependent on this relationship. Her desire to be
accepted by her peers and to have close friendships is also strong,
however she feels frustrated and unsuccessful in this area. Her
feelings about her peers were poignantly reflected in the following responses (in italics) on the Incomplete Sentences Test:

I am unhappiest when…*my friends pick on me.*

I feel sad about…*my friends, cause they pick on me and won't sit
with me.*

I lose my temper if…*my friends start hurting me and picking on
me.*

I worry about…*friends.*

On the Thematic Apperception Test, this theme was continued
in the following story:

*This girl feels lonely…she has no friends…she just lives in this
place with a mother, a father and a horse…she wishes she had friends
but she'll just be with her mother and be happy…she'll get friends
someday.*

The evidence that Allegra knew exactly what was going on makes
me well up with tears even twenty years later.

DIFFICULTY WITH SOCIAL SKILLS

Why do children with LD have such a challenging time with friendship? Usually these challenges can be attributed to problems with
social skills. A child with a language or auditory processing disorder,
for example, may have difficulty understanding what other people say
or what they mean when they say it. This same child might also have
trouble expressing ideas in speech. A child with ADHD may be impul-
sive, hyperactive, inattentive, or "spacey." This does not apply only to
the classroom. Imagine a group of children listening to a coach give
instructions for a new game. "Got it?" the coach says, and the children
nod. Then they start playing, and one child has no idea what is going
on, which obviously affects the success of her team. She has ADHD
and her mind wandered when the instructions were given out. How
will her teammates feel about that? Will they be understanding and

compassionate? Probably not. What will happen the next time sides are chosen? Chances are she will not be the first one picked.

Isolation and being "left out" can happen to any child with a disability, even to one who, by all appearances, is extremely popular and well liked.

In talking about his son Charlie's experience in high school, our Special Father John says, "Charlie was in the same grammar school from kindergarten to middle school, and everybody knew he was one of those special needs kids. When he got to the middle school, they brought kids in from six different grammar schools. Very early on, I was told that a student turned to one of his friends and said, 'Why does that kid talk so funny?' And one of the former students from Charlie's grammar school said, 'You leave him alone.' There was a circle of protection for him because he's such a nice guy.

"For the four years he was in high school, he was the manager of the football team. He was also the weatherman on the internal school TV station. He called himself Hurricane Chuck. When we went for the interview process for the Threshold Program [a college program for students with severe LD], I was talking to the program director and told him that all the other students in the high school loved Charlie dearly. He said, 'I'm sure that's all true, but how many of them ask him out on a Friday or Saturday night?' And of course, the answer is 'none.' Sure, everybody loved Charlie, but they didn't want to hang out with him. He wanted to talk about Pokémon when he was a senior in high school because that was his level. So he had a great school experience, but we had to make sure he had other things to do on the weekends and evenings so he didn't feel he was just sitting around while all his buddies were doing other things."

Does it have to be this way? What is it about our children with LD that makes them so often unsuccessful at the job of friendship?

Maybe we should start by asking if friendship is all that easy to begin with. In our development as social creatures, friendship is the way we form lasting bonds. How many of us know or hear of people who originally met in kindergarten and are still best of friends, thirty, forty, even fifty years later? Surely their lives diverged and they took up different careers or moved to different locations, but something in those early days of childhood created a bond that does not break. My very best friend today is someone I met when I was entering ninth grade at age thirteen.

Most of us learn the skills necessary to form friendships without really trying. We're not aware of learning the meaning behind such differing social cues as a smile or a frown. Our mothers might say "not so loud" once in a while if we're a little too rambunctious one day, but somewhere along the line we learn to modulate our voices to fit the occasion. We learn all the intricacies of the dance called "social skills" without having been officially taught, and therefore we find it absolutely baffling when we discover that our own child doesn't have the first clue about things that come so naturally to others.

And let's be honest about this. Yes, we are crushed by our children's lack of friends, but part of that sense of loss comes from a feeling that our child's inability to fit in influences our *own* ability to fit in. If your son is unable to join the other boys when they play, how comfortable are you going to feel when joining the mothers who are sitting on the sidelines watching them? I tried to get Allegra to participate in group activities and ended up sitting in the bleachers wearing a floppy hat I would pull down low. I was actually embarrassed by my daughter's inability to follow directions that seemed so effortless to others her age. So why did I put her in that position in the first place? For her benefit or mine?

If ever we are tempted to dismiss our child's desire to "fit in," we should recognize how strong that very desire is within ourselves.

OTHER PARENTS' PREJUDICES

Sometimes, the trouble comes from unexpected places. Our child with LD may find a perfect companion, someone who accepts him for who he is, and then we hear from that little friend's parents.

When Lisa and her family first moved to the small New England town where she now lives, she thought it would be great to get her son Ryan involved in basketball and baseball in the hope that he might make some friends. "One of the coaches happened to know my husband," she says. "His wife was talking to me about nutrition—she's a whole-foods nutritionist. It was just wonderful. But then I said to her,

'My son takes medication and it really decreases his appetite, and I wonder if you could give me some nutritional tips, for example, some type of soup that might help him put on some weight.' She asked what kind of medication, and when I told her it was for ADHD, she looked at me strangely. She didn't say much after that, but I began to notice that she didn't sit next to me so much at the games anymore. I thought something was up, but sometimes I'm a little hypersensitive about my child, so I thought I might be overreacting."

At the end of the year, Lisa went to a party at another coach's house. This coach's wife is a nurse. "We were sitting around a table," Lisa says, "and the first woman, the nutritionist, looks at me and then looks right at the nurse and says, 'You know, I think some parents overmedicate their children.' The nurse, who didn't know my son was on medication or had any problem at all, said, 'Yeah, it's like a psych ward at school.' That was it for me. I said, 'It's been lovely having been in your home,' and I collected my child and left. I haven't spoken to either of them again. She lives right down the street from me. It's really a shame. My son was good friends with her son. He had slept over at their house, they had playdates. I would certainly have let Ryan continue that friendship—in fact, I hoped they would continue. But her son never called again. It was really hurtful because he couldn't understand why he lost his friend. And, of course, I didn't tell him the real reason. He has made other friends since then, so he's doing fine. But you hate to see your child hurt like that. It's just awful."

What can we do about this? We could try to educate those parents, but let's face it: we will always find people who cannot be educated because they do not want to be educated. Their theories about LD fit neatly into their worldview, and it might not be worth the time to try to change it. Lisa says, "My feeling is this: my son has an issue, and if you have a problem with that, then that is your problem. It's not my problem, and it's not my son's problem, either. Life is too short, and there are too many other things to get done."

I agree. So let's leave aside the ignorant parent who will not let her child play with your child. That is a tough case, and if you're willing to try to change it, more power to you. Sometimes it helps to know that, for every parent out there who refuses to accept your child's LD, there is another who welcomes it. Not long after Lisa had the trouble with the nutritionist, she received a call from another mother in the neighborhood. She called Lisa out of the blue and said, "I have a personal question. If you want to hang up on me, you can." This neighbor said her son told her that Lisa's son Ryan goes down to the nurse every day to get medication, and her son does, too. She asked if Ryan had a disability, and when Lisa said yes, the neighbor said, "Oh, thank God, because my son has a disability, too, and now he thinks he can have a friend like himself!"

WHAT CAN YOU DO?

There are things we mothers can do to encourage friendships. When Allegra was younger, I spent a great deal of time teaching her the social side of life. I included her in everything. I taught her ways to make conversation, how to get by with small talk (a skill most of us find awkward, to say the least), how to listen, and how to compliment people. I taught her basic rules of etiquette, which may seem stuffy and old-fashioned to some, but for young people with poor social skills, having a set of rules to follow can be extremely helpful. Very early on, Allegra learned the value of complimenting others and, especially, *listening*. So many difficulties in interpersonal relationships can be smoothed by the simple act of listening. Those who can do it, or learn to do it, have an advantage over those who can't or won't.

For older children and young adults, I suggest trying to get them to cultivate an interest in current events and pop culture. Allegra reads two or three magazines every week, such as *Us* and *People*, and by knowing about the latest movies and celebrity gossip, she can more easily socialize with her peers. For young men, knowing about the local sports teams can often serve the same purpose. They don't have to expound on philosophy or physics—who does, these days? Most people get by with the surface details, and your child can, too.

Another important thing is to discover your child's interests and then do everything you can to help them follow those interests. It doesn't matter what they are. For Allegra, it was ice skating. It saved her self-esteem and gave a richness to her life I could never have imagined in earlier days. She found friends with similar interests. The same could happen with your child. And again, it doesn't matter what that interest is, or if it makes sense to you or not.

It is also not necessary for your child to be voted Most Popular and to have so many friends that you can't keep track of who's who. Lisa remembers asking Ryan's preschool teacher why he didn't play with the other children. The teacher said, "Ryan is going to grow up and have maybe two or three close friends who will be his friends for the rest of his life. The rest will fall by the wayside, and that's okay. And he does have a best friend now. When the class went away to Maine for a week, they bunked in the same room. They have been inseparable ever since. This boy does not have LD, but he's on Ryan's wavelength. They do goofy things together, innocent things…they'll be on the phone having singing contests with each other; they enjoy the same things. It's kind of silly, but it's innocent and it's fun. That friend 'gets' Ryan's humor, and he validates Ryan. If I could have one wish to grant to each mother, it would be for her child to find that one friend who really 'gets' her son or daughter."

Some children will not want to acknowledge that they have LD, and that's fine. I feel it makes things a whole lot easier if they do talk openly about their disability. It's one thing if a potential friend thinks your son or daughter can't read because he or she is "stupid" (and, let's face it, children are not afraid to use that word; some adults aren't, either). It's quite another thing if that same potential friend understands your child has trouble reading the list of ice cream flavors at the ice cream stand because of dyslexia. Some still won't accept it, but some definitely will.

All friendships have challenges. It takes a little work to make and keep friends, even for those of us without LD, but don't despair. There are always good-natured, open-hearted children and adults who will look beyond your child's disabilities and, as Lisa said, "get" your son or daughter.

Chapter 20

"Don't Forget About Me": Brothers and Sisters

Problems with school dominate most discussions of LD, but if I asked mothers to tell me the one issue in the home that causes the most distress or worry, I believe problems with siblings might top the list. No matter how sincerely you vow to devote equal time and attention to all your children, you cannot help devoting more time and attention to the child with LD. It becomes like a New Year's resolution you are doomed to break, and it doesn't matter how hard you try to keep it—the child with LD has a gravitational pull the other children do not and will always drag you into his or her orbit.

Many mothers are not even aware of this. If you're thinking, "Oh, that's not me. My other children know the situation and are perfectly fine with it," don't skip ahead. Trust me—I have known many mothers who feel the same and only later, when their children are adults, do they learn the truth. It comes as a shock. Just when they think they can finally sit back and put their feet up and say, "Well, I did a great job raising my child with LD," along comes one of their other children to say, "Fine, but you sure didn't do the same for me!"

I find that many adult siblings without LD truly do understand in a rational way their mother's reasons for focusing more on their brother or sister with LD, but emotionally, they still have the sense that they got the short end of the deal. It's best to stop these feelings from growing in the first place. Like everything else associated with LD, it isn't easy. It takes some effort to pull yourself away from your intense focus on the child with problems to do the same for the child without.

Mostly it's a simple matter of realizing the need is there. It means praising your child for getting straight As rather than brushing it off or ignoring the achievement for fear of making your child with LD feel insecure. It means taking time out from all the doctor appointments and school meetings to spend some time alone with your non-LD children, just to talk and to let them know that you do care, even if it seems that you are always pulled in other directions. It may mean taking the non-LD child to a doctor's appointment with you so a professional can explain the exact nature of their sibling's disorder. A child who *knows* what is going on is far more likely to accept the appearance of imbalance and partiality in the home.

This was my great mistake. Whenever Allegra's brother, Alessandro, would complain to me that Allegra was getting special treatment or that I was showing favoritism, I lashed out at him. "Maybe you would like to be her for one day" was one of my favorites. So was the ever-popular "Maybe you would like to have no friends like your sister." These gems of wisdom were *not* a good way to handle this, though I did not fully realize that until Alessandro was well into his thirties. I had asked him to speak about his experiences as the brother of someone with LD at the annual benefit for the National Center for Learning Disabilities. I was so proud to see him stroll to the stage, fully confident he would tell the assembled guests what a selfless mother I was and how I created a miraculously caring and understanding home environment for both of my children.

Not quite. He did praise me for my devotion to Allegra, but then he let me have it. I hadn't paid enough attention to him; I'd given way too much attention to Allegra; I hadn't balanced my priorities well enough; and on and on, in front of four hundred people. Awkward, yes, but he was right! He told it in a humorous, teaching way that made every mother in the audience think about her own family dynamic and whether she had managed to treat everyone fairly. Though it was painful for me to hear it, I am so appreciative of the lesson I learned that night because I have been able to pass it on to others.

A couple of years after Alessandro gave his speech, I was at dinner with Deborah (whom you met in an earlier interview), her husband, Johnny, and their daughter Sunny, who does not have LD. Their daughter Windy, who has LD, was not there that night. I talked about Alessandro's speech, and how it made me realize I could have done things a little better, and then I turned to Sunny and asked, "Did you have the same sort of feelings growing up?"

Exactly the same thing happened. Deborah and Johnny were stunned to hear Sunny speak openly for the first time about the difficulty of being a sibling of a child with LD and how it felt not to have been treated fairly.

Do not assume your children without LD understand what you are going through or why it is necessary for you to spend so much time on your child with LD. It took Alessandro and Sunny years to be able to open up about past hurts and feelings of injustice. They carried those feelings for a long time, and still do. Do not allow your children to do the same.

SUNNY AND WINDY

When Deborah talked about Sunny, she said, "She's just like her name. She's bright sunshine. She was a straight-A student, and it was always difficult, because we could never celebrate Sunny the way she needed to be celebrated. It just brings tears to my eyes, because I'm sure there were times when my energy went in unequal ways to Windy. I had to be there for school. I had to go into her classroom. I never let up with Windy. A mother has to be like that. And because Sunny was competent and could do things, she was overlooked. I'm sure there were times when I didn't give her the attention she needed. I expected things out of her that I didn't expect out of Windy. So I'm not sure I handled that well at all."

Deborah knows she didn't handle it well, but notice that she also touched upon that central reality: "I never let up with Windy. A mother has to be like that."

She's right. A mother *does* have to be like that. She has to fight for her child with LD and never give up, but at the same time, she must try as hard as she can to make sure the other children don't feel left out.

Right after I spoke with Deborah, Sunny—now thirty-four and married with two children—agreed to talk to me about sibling issues. Deborah didn't want to stay, for fear it would make Sunny hold back on some of her feelings, but Sunny insisted that she stay. "There isn't anything you haven't heard," she said, and Deborah reluctantly sat down again.

The first thing I can say is that Deborah's description of Sunny as a ray of sunshine is accurate. She is smart, articulate, and bubbling with fun and good humor. If some of the things she says may sound a bit harsh, let me assure you they were said with a self-deprecating laugh and deep appreciation of her mother.

I asked her when she first become aware there might be a problem with her sister.

"I can pinpoint it exactly," she said. "I was in first grade and she was in second or third grade. We were in the bathtub together doing simple multiplication tables. The babysitter was asking Windy, 'What's three times three?' I was two years younger than Windy, so I obviously didn't know the answer. But they were doing multiplication in Windy's class and she didn't know the answer, either. She kept saying 'two,' and the babysitter kept saying, 'No, it's not.' After about the fifth time, I said, 'Windy, it's nine. She gave you the answer five times! It's *nine*.' I remember thinking, 'Wait...I'm understanding something that Windy, who is my older sister, can't understand.'"

"How did that make you feel?"

"I remember being confused. At that age, a child has no perception of the big picture. Everything for a child is here and now and immediate, and I think you need to get a little older before you really understand what is happening."

"Sometimes siblings can't understand learning disabilities," I said, "especially when it's the older brother or sister who has LD."

"Right. I remember saying that out loud: 'Windy, what's wrong with you?' I didn't even understand what multiplication was, but after hearing the answer over and over, I knew the answer was nine."

"Did you see other things?"

"More than anything, I saw emotional situations. There were two standards for how we behaved emotionally in our house. My younger brother John and I were brought up with one set of standards and Windy was brought up with another. She was allowed to get away with things that we were not. She would cry and she could talk back to

Mom and say things that John and I would never dream of saying. We knew from an early age that that just was not the way you do things, and somehow Windy was allowed to do it. She would get upset and didn't know how to verbalize properly.

"There were other things, too, little things. When she was in the middle grades, she would take my toothbrush, or if I wore a new sweater, the next thing I knew, Windy would be wearing it. If I went to my mother and told her she took my brand-new sweater, my mother would say, 'She's different, she's special, just let her wear it.' But I would never have been able to do that to Windy or John."

"Did you feel a sense of unfairness?"

"Of course! On Saturday, before we could go out and play, we all had to clean our rooms. Windy would take the cover and just throw it over the bed, while John and I would work for thirty minutes organizing our shoes and our closets. Windy could go right out and play within three seconds, but we had to stay there. We'd say, 'Mom, how come Windy can go out and play?' and the answer would be, 'Because Windy's special.' Over and over, those were the words I heard: 'Windy is special.' Well, what does that make me? *Not* special? I thought I was doing everything right, but Windy is special. In my particular situation, I had a younger brother who was the apple of my father's eye, and my mother was so focused on Windy because she was special, so I think I have a classic case of Middle Child Syndrome. Honestly, it wasn't until Windy left for school that a lot of people said I finally came out of my shell and got to talk and speak. I wasn't scared anymore."

"Scared?" I asked, thinking that was a peculiar reaction to having a sibling with LD. "What scared you?"

"I kept thinking I was doing something wrong. I really did. I thought there was something wrong with me."

"Did your mother ever sit down and tell you exactly what was going on?"

"I knew enough to know that she was hurting, so I didn't want to bring it up. She would say 'Windy is special' or 'Windy is not like you,' but she was still trying to figure it out herself. She didn't know what was wrong with Windy, either. But as a child your world is black and white. You want to know what is wrong, and my parents didn't have a definitive answer. My mother would say, 'Windy has a different way of learning.' She was trying so hard to avoid saying that Windy was less than anyone else, because that was not the case. Windy was never less than anyone else."

"She used the word *special?*" I said.

"Yes. It's an incredible word, now that I think about it. What a great word to define her, because she *is* special. Yes, she is a little bit different, but she is special."

I turned to Deborah and asked if she remembered Sunny asking her why Windy could go out and play when she couldn't.

"Yes, I do remember that," Deborah said. "We had just gone through a week of turmoil with Windy's school, and I knew Windy was suffering, and I thought, 'I can't come down on her again. Everybody had been coming down on her.' I always felt that she needed someplace where she could be safe and could be free, where she could be herself. Also, I didn't know how much to expect out of Windy. What was her best effort? I didn't know that. For example, could she make her bed the same way that Sunny and John could? I wanted our home to be a place where she was safe and wouldn't feel discouraged because she couldn't do it like everyone else. It was a place where her best was accepted."

"I feel the same way you do," I said.

"I could cry," Deborah said, reaching for a tissue. "I *am* crying. I know I didn't do the right things."

"But you can't beat yourself up about it," I said, knowing my words would have little effect.

Deborah's voice trembled: "But here was this child, Sunny, who had straight As and we couldn't celebrate her the way she should have been celebrated."

"There were things that had to be put on hold," Sunny said. "For example, when I turned sixteen, I wanted to get my driver's license. Everyone does when they turn sixteen. Mom didn't want me to get my driver's license because she was afraid it would hurt Windy's feelings. I think that might have been the first time I put my foot down. I said, 'I'm not going to give up my driver's license because of Windy's feelings.' I had put everything on hold for so long for Windy. At the same time, looking back at it now as a mother, I don't know what I would have done differently. With this perspective I can look back and say my mother did the best she could. I don't think there is any way to please two or three people in that situation. But when you're that age, it's very hard to grasp 'she is special and you're not.'"

By trying to shield the feelings of one child, a parent can't help but hurt the other. I made many mistakes exactly like this one. I was so concerned with Allegra's feelings that I often neglected or ignored Alessandro's. I used to beg him to take Allegra out with his friends when we were skiing. We were usually with relatives, so I didn't think it would be too embarrassing for him, but now looking back on it, why should he want to take his younger sister along? I don't think it has as much to do with her LD as with the fact that she was six years younger, but I didn't want to see Allegra left out once again. "No mother actively ignores one of her children," I said to Deborah and Sunny, "but certainly the focus on the child with LD makes it appear that way."

Sunny agreed. "That's right. In our house it was a matter of 'let's have family meetings about how to deal with Windy.' I had to go see a counselor because Windy had problems with me. So I went to a counselor to talk about Windy. Windy went to a counselor. Our family went to a counselor. It all centered on Windy. But more than anything, I want to get this across: these days Windy truly is my best friend. We talk constantly on the telephone, sometimes five times a day on the weekends. She calls every single night to check up on the kids. I appreciate her so much. We plan our vacations so Windy can go with us. In the future, when we go to Disney World with the kids, it will be great because Windy will be more than happy to take them on It's a Small World twenty times. She loves it! And we love having her around. So thankfully I don't have a resentment that is going to last the rest of my life."

"I find that's the case with many adult siblings," I said. "Once they are mature enough to see and understand their brother or sister's problem, they become much more accepting of their own past. Of course, others never come to terms with it and carry their resentments long into adulthood. When the siblings are young, they often have a sense that they can't do anything to get their parents to pay attention to them. They try so hard, they achieve more, they strive more, but they still never get the recognition."

"That's true," Sunny said. "My husband told me recently that I'm still clamoring for their attention. I sometimes feel that all my life was spent jumping up and down and shouting, 'Hello! I'm here!' Every time I did something that I thought warranted a response of 'That's great!' I didn't get it. They would say, 'That's good,' and then turn to Windy and say, 'Oh, Windy, you took two steps—that's *great!*"

I asked Sunny what she would say to a mother who is going through this with her own children.

"I thought about this a lot because I don't know how my mother could have done things much differently. But for one thing, I would never tell one child he or she is special and somehow make the other one feel he or she is not special. I would also sit down and talk to the sibling one-on-one."

"That's good advice," I said.

"It wasn't until Windy left home and my mother and I started traveling together and spending time alone together that I realized that I actually *was* special in her eyes, but in a different way than Windy. I would definitely recommend spending some one-on-one time with the other children and let them know that they are really as special and important as the child with LD, even if you think they already know that. Another thing that's important is to be honest about the situation. For example, you could say, 'I am so thrilled with your straight As, and I am so proud of you for your accomplishments; sometimes I don't get to tell you as much because I worry that your sister is not able to do that.'"

"Parents may think their other children won't understand, but I think they do—maybe not completely, but at some level they will understand and accept the situation," I said. "I always tell parents that I wish I had brought Alessandro to one of Allegra's doctor appointments so the doctor could explain Allegra's LD. My son had a similar situation to yours, though he was the older one. He saw Allegra getting special attention, and I never told him why, not in a way that he could understand. That's something I regret very much. Do you still harbor any feelings of jealousy toward Windy?"

"Not at all," Sunny said. "I don't think there is one part of me that is jealous of Windy. We grew up in an ideal family situation, or at least the popular idea of an ideal family: two parents, a nice house, three kids, a dog. Windy has helped broaden my perspective on life and what we consider to be ideal."

"What would you say Windy has brought to your life as the sibling of someone with LD?"

"I can answer that two ways," Sunny said. "As a child she brought the realization that things aren't always as easy as they may appear from the outside. There were some hard times that I didn't understand. It was complicated and it was stressful, and I didn't like the way I felt about her. I didn't want her around. I walked around embarrassed for about four years."

"And then you felt guilty about being embarrassed," I said.

"Yes. I thought she was always slightly off and weird, and I didn't know why, because no one really explained it to me. So she was weird, she didn't act her age, and I remember shutting down and not talking about it."

"How old were you in this period?"

"Probably from eleven to fifteen. So that's the first way I can talk about what Windy brought to my life. At that age it seemed she brought only difficulties and embarrassment. The second way I can talk about what she has brought to my life is as an adult. She brings clarity to everything I do. Things are black and white with her. If you look at things from Windy's perspective, it can simplify things."

"Do you think she's given you a heightened sense of compassion for others?"

"Absolutely! I don't think people who don't have a sibling or family member with a disability have the same sort of patience or understanding."

"I feel the same thing," I said. "I believe a person with disabilities brings value to everyone else in the family. It allows you to see that people aren't perfect, and that families aren't perfect."

"Windy was maid of honor in my wedding, and I had friends who said it was so sweet of me to include her. My attitude was that it had nothing to do with being sweet or not—she's my sister!"

"The first time you spoke about your feelings with your parents was the night I was talking about Alessandro telling me how badly I handled the situation. I asked you if you had the same feelings, and it all just came flooding out."

"Yes. I think that was the first time anyone had ever asked me anything about it. Everyone always asks Mom how she dealt with everything, or they'll ask her if it was hard on her. I *know* it was hard on her, but that was the first time anyone ever asked me, 'Was it hard on you, too?'"

Then Deborah said, "There was a lot that I wasn't aware of. But as I said before, I always worried about Sunny, and I always felt like I was held back from letting her know how much I adored her. I couldn't be as close to her as I wanted because I had to focus on this issue. I was lonely, and I didn't have anybody else to help me, so it was almost like saying to my husband, 'You take Sunny and I'll take Windy.'"

"It's a very hard issue for all of us," I said. "That's why I want to bring it to people's attention. I've talked to some parents who say, 'Oh, no, there's no problem with my other children.' And I say, 'Don't be so sure of that—go home and *talk* to them!'"

Deborah said she wished she had talked to Sunny earlier. "I didn't know it was this hard on her."

"Were you relieved once the air was cleared," I asked, "or has it become more of a burden for you?"

"Both," Deborah said. "It was additional affirmation that it was a painful journey for her as well. I didn't know the extent of it. But I always feel that we're better if we can just get things out and we can talk about them and be open with each other."

"And some mothers get used to the idea that they are the only one involved," I said. "They become obsessed because they have to be. But then you get these additional burdens down the road. You learn that you didn't pay enough attention to your other children, and you can start to beat yourself up for being too much of an advocate. Even when you think the problems are almost over, another one comes along. That's why you see elderly women in some of the learning disabilities organizations—they're still obsessed with a child who's forty or fifty years old!"

"It's not the same with most men," Sunny said. "If you asked my father right now, he would say, 'There's no problem. Sunny was always fine.' I love Dad wholeheartedly, but he just doesn't understand. He would just laugh it off."

"He doesn't get below the surface of it because he can't understand," I said. "And for the mother, there seems to be nothing she can do to heal the pain. She's *always* below the surface."

"That's right," Deborah said. "And in one sense, this is where my faith comes in. I feel like Windy has taught us more and changed our family dynamic, and that we are finer people because of Windy. And when I see how Windy is now, independent and happy, it's a miracle to me. I don't mean she doesn't have down days and that there aren't challenges, but it's a miracle to me that she's on her own. So in some ways it has been a blessing. It is a 'road less traveled,' but one with deep rewards. As painful as this has been for all of us, it's been a blessing in the sense that I feel we are all more human, more compassionate, and more understanding of people."

"Was your faith strong before all of this?"

"I had faith, but not as strong," Deborah said. "Windy's situation sent me to my knees. I longed to be there for her in so many ways, and yet I felt as if I didn't have the skills I needed. I had this enormous sense of responsibility to provide for her. I prayed a lot…for wisdom and discernment, for guidance, for the right professional support, the right schools, the right teachers and tutors, the right activities, and for friends for her. You see, our other two children were bright and gifted, and were so involved in their schools. They were leaders and had loads of friends. We were close and they knew I believed in them, and there was a sense of stability in their lives. Windy's situation made me even more grateful for them and who they were, but with Windy, it was like a broken dream. All my expectations for her had to be different, and I was still learning what and how much to expect.

"She was constantly changing schools and teachers, and she was always having to make new friends. And so I knew my role was different with Windy, and that she needed even more stable support, and that she needed to be reinforced even more, and that I believed in her as well. I felt that if Windy could sense and feel accepted, and be affirmed for who she was, and that if I could encourage her for the gifts and goodness inside of her, that she could carry that sense with her for the rest of her life. It was Windy, and walking this path, that made me say, 'I don't understand all this, but I have to trust.' We are all different people now. We were changed by this experience. I don't think we would have had the depth of character if it hadn't been for Windy. She is a blessing. And I am grateful to her. She taught me so much about life."

"I completely agree," said Sunny. "My sister made me who I am."

JAMES AND CHARLIE

When LD is diagnosed in a family member, it can come as an unwelcome shock and be viewed as a burden or a stroke of terrible luck. You may be feeling that right now, and wondering how it will affect your children without LD. Looking at it from the long view, I now see that most of us eventually come to the realization that LD did not damage our families beyond repair—far from it! We see how it has enriched our lives in ways we never imagined. We also see how it has instilled compassion in our children without LD, and given them a sense of greater purpose and a better understanding of imperfections. They come to realize that not everyone is the same, and not everyone is perfect. It frees them from superficial concerns and allows them to look at people as they really are, with all their faults and weakness, and all their strengths.

I met a young man named James who gave a speech at his graduation from middle school. His older brother Charlie was born with learning disabilities. Both young men are the sons of John, whom you read about in the Special Fathers chapter.

James had many topics to choose from for his graduation speech: he could have spoken about sports, or a favorite teacher, or his friends, but this 12-year-old boy chose a different topic. This is his speech in its entirety.

Charlie
by James L.

I wait in extended day for my mom to pick me up. I see a tall, lanky figure with big, black Velcro shoes. Oh no, not Charlie. I try to pretend like I don't know him.

"Yo bro, Mom's waiting for you. Let's go," he shouts.

I ignore him.

"Yo Jimbo, come on."

I quickly walk and tug him along, trying to get out of there as quickly as possible.

"Hey James, who's that?" somebody asks.

I quickly slide in front of him, blocking his shoes. I try to say something, but no words were coming out of my mouth. Charlie interrupts.

"I'm his older brother. The name's Charlie. Nice to meet you."

"Nice to meet you, too."

I step away, no longer blocking his shoes. The kid didn't care and that's when I realized that I shouldn't care, either.

The thing that I will remember most about our school is that everyone accepts each other, no matter how different they are. I am no longer embarrassed of Charlie.

I am proud to call him my brother.

Chapter 21

How Are You Doing?:
Taking Care of Yourself

"How is your son doing?" a neighbor might ask, or maybe a coworker will ask if your daughter is doing better in school. Your mother might express her worries about your child's progress, and then your mother-in-law will go on and on about how all this LD stuff is taking a toll on her son. Rare is the friend, neighbor, or family member who puts aside the effects of "all this LD stuff" on others and turns to you to ask: "And how are *you* doing?"

For all our talk about a child's self-esteem or the necessity of a father to come to terms with his child's LD, we don't often hear about the mother's state of mind. She is, after all, the one who most often takes on the majority of the burdens. She is the one who spends hour after sleepless hour worrying about the outcome of an evaluation. She takes her child to soccer practice and stands on the sideline, her heart aching as she watches her son or daughter try to fit in. Most of all, she feels that all this stress and worry are simply a part of her "job," that it all comes with the territory, and that she has no right to complain about the toll it has taken on her. "Too selfish," she thinks, or "Yes, but what are my problems when compared to my child's?"

On top of this, many mothers must contend with the darker, more negative emotions that flash through their minds, such as anger, embarrassment, and shame. I well remember feeling embarrassed at times by something Allegra did or said when she was a child, and then being overwhelmed by a wave of shame and guilt for feeling embarrassed. Another mother I spoke to said she sometimes feels a surge of anger during homework sessions and has all she can do not to shout, "For God's sake, why can't you get this? You just *had* it a minute ago!"—and then, like me, immediately retreats into shame and guilt, even though her anger had never been expressed to anyone but herself.

We all feel these things at one time or another. We wouldn't be human if we didn't. Usually these feelings arise because of an awareness of others. "What are they thinking?" we might ask ourselves, or "What if they talk about my child to someone else?"

I asked Deborah, one of our Special Mothers, about this: "Did you ever feel embarrassed about Windy? Or guilty?"

"Maybe at some point I did," she said. "I don't remember feeling embarrassed as much as I felt that others didn't understand Windy."

"Did anyone ever say anything to you that was hurtful or insensitive?"

"Oh, yes! But I try not to remember things like that. I just went through an experience when a group of mothers were talking about their various experiences raising their children. They called it 'the peaks and the valleys' of raising a child, how some days were great and others not so great. As they were talking, I realized that, with Windy, her childhood seemed to have many times in the valley."

"Meaning what?"

"Meaning that there were times that the journey was painful. We all have peaks and valleys in our lives, but with Windy there was often a lot of pain involved. But as time went on, with friends, the right schools, good support, her work, she has come to have real peace. She is such a positive person. She's got the purest heart. I called her my Child of Courage then, always facing the challenges with courage and inner strength. She is the most thoughtful and loving person, and so real. There is no pretense with Windy."

"I meet mothers who still carry the pain of their children's LD long after those children became adults," I said. "I am one of them. I will never truly get over the pain of those early days. Do you feel the same?"

"I do," Deborah said, "but, in one sense, I'm also grateful for those days because they made us all stronger people. Today I look back and see that Windy has come such a long way."

"Is it continual pain even now? Or do you think the pain is left over from those early traumatic days, and you just can't get over it?"

"Oh, there is still pain, but maybe the pain is mostly mine rather than hers...I don't know. Of course, I want Windy to have everything others have. I would love for her to have somebody to marry and children of her own. She loves children and her work is now with children. I would love for her to have all those things, but I don't know if it will happen. On the other hand, she truly is happy. She has close friends. She has her independence. She has such common sense, and she's living a happier life than I ever imagined. I'm so proud of her."

"How often do you talk to her?"

"Every morning and every night. Usually twice or three times a day. I love being with her."

"Is there any further advice you would give to another mother just starting out on this journey?"

"Oh, yes, and when I'm asked, I share these three things, and I guess they're true about mothers and all children. First, be attuned to who your child is and not who you want your child to be. Love your child for just who they are. If they have a particular interest, encourage it because it may end up being their gift to the world. Second, be their mother and not their teacher. Of course, all mothers naturally teach their children, but what I mean is that we should be more interested in their person and in building their character than in their performance. Others can be their academic teacher. I believe that each child needs to have one person who believes in them, accepts and affirms them, who loves them just the way they are, and wants to encourage the gifts and goodness, maybe even the uniqueness that is within them. I believe that role is for the mother. No one else can give the constant love, continued interest and encouragement, and that important support the way a mother can. Third, be their best advocate. No one will love or understand your child the way you do. So always be their best advocate. It takes constant attention. Persevere always. Keep believing in that child, and never, *ever* give up."

I would add to those words of wisdom, "And be sure to take care of yourself."

HOW TO FOCUS ON YOUR NEEDS

We must not fall into the trap of thinking that concern for ourselves somehow takes away or lessens our concern for our children. We mothers of children with LD have enough concern and worry to blanket the world. Surely, we can spare a little for ourselves!

Sometimes the pressures build and have no outlet, but they cannot stay bottled up forever. They eventually come out, but in ways that are not productive and can actually harm our family. Some of the mothers I have talked to are overwhelmed. They can no longer cope with the uncertainty and frustrations brought about by a diagnosis of their child's LD.

One mother I met, Marianne, certainly had experience with this. She has two sons, Peter and Andrew. The older one, Peter, was diagnosed with dyslexia and ADHD when he was ten years old. She told me the pressures of dealing with her son's LD caused her to have what she called "a bit of a nervous breakdown."

"You really have to work to keep balance in your life," Marianne told me. "For me, that means not always focusing on my son. If I *always* focus on him, I can get myself into an obsessive state. It sounds corny but one of the things that helps me stay really balanced is watching *The Dog Whisperer*. The dog trainer on that show, Cesar Millan, is a bit of a psychologist, too, for both dogs and their owners. He always says you don't get the dog you want; you get the dog you need. I think that philosophy spills over into other aspects of your life, because it's all about energy. I try to bring his theory into human affairs. For example, he advises against escalating situations in which you try to match or surpass the other person's anger or negative energy. It's always about being calm and steady and projecting the same sort of energy you would like to receive from others. When you do, other people react to it. You can also try that with children or with anyone. For example, I used to get very angry. Someone would say something and I would say something back, or I'd try to top them. But now I just let it go, and that helps me stay balanced. It's a process. I also have to walk every morning. I have to get exercise."

Exercise is a key to many women's ability to handle the stress of LD. Meditation is another. Mothers who would never dream of meditating or taking up yoga now swear by it as the antidote to the pressures brought on by LD. Others talk to a therapist. Some of you might click your tongue and say, "Meditation? Yoga? Therapy? I could never focus so much on myself!"

Think of it this way: by focusing on your own needs, you create the ability to focus much more strongly and effectively on everyone else's needs. In the cause of ensuring your child is getting the best help possible, taking care of yourself should be considered as important and necessary as attending a school meeting or taking your child to a pediatrician. You cannot be helpful if you are continually overwhelmed by the million and one emotions that come flooding over us, especially in the early days of a child's diagnosis.

When another of our Special Mothers, Helen, felt overwhelmed by her son's diagnosis and lack of progress, she started seeing a therapist. "I was completely consumed by my son's LD," she said. "I couldn't make decisions—none!"

"Decisions about your son?" I asked.

"I couldn't make *any* decisions. Little, everyday decisions. And I was so preoccupied that I would go to bed at night, sleep for a couple of hours, and then wake up and be up all night worrying about things that did not need to be worried about."

"Things to do with school?" I asked.

"No," she said. "Ridiculous things, like 'Oh, I really need to get that bowl back from her.' Completely insane things that did not need to be obsessed about at four a.m.! That kind of behavior is just not me. I never worried about things like that."

"Why do you think you did it?" I asked.

"I felt so powerless about the things that were happening at the school. I felt such a lack of control that I was grasping at things that I *could* control. But then I would get up and go through the day and nothing was getting accomplished, so the cycle started all over again. Most of this happened when my son moved to a new school in first grade. In his kindergarten he'd been getting counseling and I felt he was moving toward something, but nothing was happening in the new school. I felt helpless. I was consumed by the fact that nothing was getting done and there was nothing I could do about it."

"And your reaction was to obsess about things you might be able to control," I said.

"Yes. Looking back on it now, I think that's what it was. But at the time, I just thought I was losing my mind. I *knew* it was insane to act the way I was acting. It was completely irrational. I was up at night, all night, worrying about things that I normally couldn't care less about. I was miserable, and at one point I thought I was miserable because of my marriage, though that wasn't really the problem at all. I didn't know what the problem was, but I knew I had to do something. I couldn't live like that. I went to a therapist who introduced me to meditation, and I joined a meditation class. At first I thought, 'Oh, this is ridiculous.' That was just not me. But I decided to try it. I was amazed by how much it cleared my mind."

"Is that when you realized it wasn't your marriage?" I asked.

"Yes! And also, I had to remove myself from the negative thinking of others. A friend of mine was in the same boat I was, and we were living in this negative view of things. So I removed myself from her a little bit. I had to. I was consumed and surrounded by negative thinking, and I realized I had to snap out of it."

"You really had to be proactive about it," I said. "You had to step up and say, 'I need to change something.'"

"Yes. I realized I needed to change something because I was miserable, and to some extent it was affecting my marriage because I was consumed with it. This is something that might be helpful to someone going through it now. When I found out about my son's dyslexia, I talked to a neighbor who also had a son with LD and she casually said, 'You should be careful because these things can really affect a marriage.' At the time I thought, 'What is she talking about?' I thought she was a little crazy, and I thought, 'How could it possibly affect a marriage?' But that little remark really helped me later on when I remembered what she said. It also helped that my husband saw the whole picture before I did. At first he was in denial about our son's LD, but then he moved right into accepting it. He didn't go through the middle part like I did. But he also had the luxury of putting it all on me. He would say, 'All right, you figure out what's best,' and that was nice because he trusted me to do it."

Marianne said, "I make the majority of the decisions, too. It's not that my husband doesn't want to be involved, but he works all day. I work all day, too, but I work from home. My husband trusts my judgment."

"That is a huge thing, a positive thing," Helen said. "At the same time, it can bring on a lot of stress. It makes you feel that, ultimately, you are responsible. And sometimes I think, 'Oh, my God, what if I ruin him!?'"

I turned to Marianne and said, "Earlier you described what you went through as having a bit of a nervous breakdown. How did that happen and what did you experience?"

"I think it happened because I was newly married, my son Peter was my first child, and I wanted everything to be perfect. I burnt myself out. I tried so hard to be Martha Stewart. I was a stay-at-home mom, so I always made dinner at five o'clock and had the house looking perfect, spotless. All of Peter's food was organic at home and all his baby food was homemade."

"Oh, God help you," Helen interjected with a laugh.

"I know!" Marianne said. "It wasn't easy. I joined a Mommy and Me play group. I read every book I could find about early childhood. I started to watch other people's children so I could compare. I tried to be perfect, and part of that was because I was fighting the secret thought that my child *wasn't* perfect. So if I tried hard enough to be perfect, no one would know that he wasn't. They would think that because I'm the mom who has all the playdates, and I'm the mom whose house is always clean, and I'm the mom who makes the dinners. As a result, I burnt myself out."

"You couldn't keep up the facade," I said.

"No. And that's exactly what it was, a facade. I was always angry with my husband. He was working two jobs because we were newly married, with a new house and a baby, and he was stressed—but I was mad at him because he didn't understand and because he wasn't home. But he was working two jobs! I couldn't appreciate that, because I had this kid who wouldn't stop crying. It perpetuated itself and finally I just couldn't do it anymore. I just shut down."

"How so?" I asked.

"Everything fell apart," Marianne said. "The facade crumbled. I wouldn't clean. I wouldn't get out of bed."

"Did it happen suddenly?"

"Yes. One day I woke up and I realized I didn't want to get out of bed and do that anymore. I never felt like I wanted to hurt myself or hurt anybody—I just didn't want to participate in my life. I opted out. I stayed in bed. The house fell apart. The laundry didn't get done. My husband became frustrated and angry, and that was certainly understandable. That was *my* job. He couldn't work two jobs and then cook and clean and take care of the kids. He got angrier and angrier."

"Who took care of your son?" I asked.

"I did. But that was all I was doing. I was going through the motions. I was the perfect mom for two years, and then I had my second child, Andrew—and that's when it really started to decline. Having the second baby was just the final straw. I realized I just couldn't be this fake, perfect person. I'd thought if I tried hard enough, Peter would get better, but he just never did, and I thought, 'Am I going to be like this forever?' It was an overwhelming idea."

I asked Marianne how she overcame it.

"I think you have to hit rock bottom," she said. "It's like anything else in your life. The moment you move toward change is usually the moment when you've decided it is just too painful to keep the status quo."

"Did your husband help?"

"Yes, but there was a point when he couldn't help, because he was angry, too, and he was hurt, too. And he was scared! He had two little children, and his wife wasn't there mentally. He would say to me, 'Listen, you have responsibilities. You have a job, and you can't lay down on the job.' Eventually I started on the path toward recovery, but it was a slow process. It was at this point in my life that I first decided to start focusing on what would make me happy as opposed to what made me unhappy. Therapy played a part, and I went back to work part-time. It sounds odd, but working outside the home was good for me. I didn't feel like a failure in the professional world, and that sense of well-being carried over at home. I stopped being so self-critical and, with the support of my husband, things improved to the point where I could take on even more than I ever could have before."

THIS TOO SHALL PASS

You have just heard from two women who tell harrowing tales of their lives spinning out of control. It's important for you to know that today Helen and Marianne are accomplished professionals, reliable and level-headed, without a hint of what one of them called the "temporary insanity" that once brought them to their knees. The symptoms they describe—inability to get out of bed, trouble making decisions, losing interest in everyday activities—are classic symptoms of depression. If you feel any of these things, do not hesitate to ask for help. It does not matter how strong you are, or how even-keeled. LD can blindside you and lead you into places and beliefs and thought patterns you never imagined possible. Do not shrug your shoulders and sigh and resign yourself to this new debilitating way of life.

Everyone in the LD world knows of at least one parent who obsesses about her child's LD or the school or a particular teacher to the exclusion of all other topics of conversation. We can see how it gnaws at her. We hear the bitterness in her voice. We know instinctively that her behavior and obsessions cannot possibly be healthy for her family or her child. We imagine the teacher cringing when she sees this person's face at the door, once again coming in to harangue and accuse. And most of all, we think, "Thank heavens I'm not like that."

It's good to be thankful, but don't be surprised if you find yourself in a similar predicament someday. Sometimes we are not aware of it until later. Step back, get some balance in your life, ask yourself, "Am I handling this well? Am I handling it at all?" If you feel you are not, but see no way out of the obsessive spiral, make an appointment to speak with a professional. If you are reluctant to do that, talk to a friend or sympathetic family member (but it will do no good to approach a family member who has already told you that you're overprotective and that your child is fine, you're imagining things, etc.).

Don't keep it to yourself. Find help.

You need it. You deserve it.

EPILOGUE
Role of a Lifetime: Becoming Your Child's Advocate

I'd like to tell you a final story before we part ways.

If you have read my previous books or ever heard me speak at a learning disabilities conference, you already know this story. I tell it every time I speak. I'm not obsessed by it. It's just that when I look back over my life, I always circle back to this particular day as the one that changed the course and direction of my life more than any other.

As I mentioned in an earlier chapter, when Allegra was in her second year of nursery school, the headmistress at her school suggested that I have her evaluated for "learning problems." That didn't sound like a serious issue to me. I thought the term might indicate a problem with attention span, or maybe a short lag in reading ability. When the headmistress then hinted that Allegra might have trouble in a regular kindergarten, my internal alarm bells began to clang—not loudly, but with a definite steady beat. "What did she mean by that?" I wondered.

Rather than wallow in uncertainty, I decided to go to the top. I found someone who, at that time, was regarded as the top pediatric neurologist in New York City. Surely, he would tell me whether or not anything was wrong. I remained confident that the headmistress's fears were overstated, and that those muffled alarm bells would be silenced. He would say, "She has a minor problem with her attention span, but it is nothing that won't work itself out in time," and then he would hand me his bill. Done. On to kindergarten.

I took Allegra to his office to be tested. He did not do the testing himself, but used his vast knowledge to study the results and make his pronouncements. When the time came, he asked me to meet with him. I sat in his office as he looked over the reports, spread out on his shiny mahogany desk. There was no small talk. No pleasant chitchat. He said nothing until he looked up at me and in a cold, professional voice said, "From these results it is clear that your daughter is severely mentally retarded." Before that could even sink in, he continued with, "and I feel that the best thing for you, for your daughter, and for your family is to institutionalize her." He then told me that he knew of an appropriate facility outside *London* that would take my five-year-old daughter, and though he wished he could be of further help, he was "just too busy."

Clang, clang, clang—the alarm bells were now ringing so loudly that I could hear nothing else, I could think of nothing else. I walked back to my apartment, stunned and unable to process the information I had just received. She was five! As far as I (or anyone else) was concerned, she was a happy, healthy, vibrant little girl. Institutionalized? Impossible!

We give the professionals so much power. We trust them. We believe they are using their hard-won knowledge to guide us onto the right pathways. Part of me couldn't help believing him: he was a highly regarded doctor, after all. But a larger part of me rebelled, and I knew at once that I would never follow his suggestions. I would not even accept them. He turned out to be wrong, of course. Horribly wrong about everything—about Allegra's diagnosis, her treatment, and most of all, the course of her future.

That day has remained with me for more than thirty years. I walked into that office an innocent young mother with no clear goals for my life. I walked out an advocate, though I didn't know it at the time. I left his office as a quivering, panicked young woman, certain that one of her two precious children was suddenly threatened by things she didn't understand, things that would affect her future and maybe even her life. I saw no way out. I saw no help on the horizon. I knew no one I could turn to. My family wouldn't understand. Friends had troubles of their own. And professionals? Well, I had just seen where that could lead. I did not know how to get out of the dire predicament, yet I knew I had to. I had to get out. I had to get Allegra out. I had to help her, no matter what, no matter how.

From that time forward, day by day, sometimes hour by hour, I reached out for help—tentative and unsure at first, and later with much more confidence. I did talk to family members, and they were much more supportive and understanding than I expected. Friends came along to lighten the burden. I found other professionals who were far less traumatizing and far more helpful. And eventually I found the sturdiest, most irreplaceable source of support of all: other mothers of children with special needs. Mothers like you.

Advocacy is not always something we choose in life. Often it is thrust upon us, and sometimes it happens in dreadful, alarming ways. We may be going along, happy in our careers and our role as mom, confident that nothing lies before us but sunny days and open roads— and then, as I earlier quoted my friend as saying, you feel like someone has suddenly put a gun to your head and forced you off the highway onto a dark and lonely road.

Often the first exit off that dark and lonely road is called Advocacy, and most of us cannot get there without first going through those rough, dark, isolated stretches.

The mothers you have met in this book have learned many lessons as they traveled these lonely roads. The main thing they have realized is that they—not the teacher, not the pediatrician, not the kindly neighbor—are the main pillars of support in the lives of their children. That's not to say a teacher can't come along who could make a profound difference, but no one loves your child as much as you do. No one can summon the same hyper-focus and interest in your child's future. No one will be there to support your child the way you can. And no one can ever match the depth of feeling you experience when you say to your son or daughter, "I believe in you."

A dictionary definition of *advocate* is "one who fights for another." As mothers, we were born to do this. Maternal instinct makes advocates of us all. We have a primal urge to protect our children and that is what we do from day one. But for those of us who have a child with a disability, day one goes on for a very long time.

Every mother (and father) I spoke to for this book has become an advocate in some form or other. Helen, for instance, was already an attorney, but her experience with her son Michael has compelled her to shift her professional focus to that of legal advocate. Lisa has started a business related to Special Education. Dana and Janie have become local experts in their children's disabilities, and have become far more involved in their school. Deborah and John have both joined the board of directors of the National Center for Learning Disabilities. Candace Cortiella is director of the Advocacy Institute, but was once a confused and fearful mother, just like us

All of the mothers in this book were once confused and fearful. None of them ever expected that their experience could inspire another mother, nor did they ever think that one day someone might turn to them for advice. That's what happens. We pass from fear to confidence, from confusion to knowledge; and eventually we find ourselves able to pass on to others the hard-won lessons we have learned.

That does not mean the difficulties are over for us, or that no further challenges lie ahead. We continue to learn every day. We continue to struggle. We understand that there are various paths to follow. We could follow one and become an effective fighter for the rights of our child. We could follow another and become an obsessive-compulsive nag whose every action sets our children's progress back a notch or two. The choice is ours.

I heard this recently: "If you are climbing a mountain, you hope to find rocky places and rough spots. If the mountain was completely smooth, you could not climb higher."

Our lives are like that, aren't they? The trials and troubles we face may seem as daunting as a high cliff, but if everything we did was smooth as silk, we would forever remain on the low ground and never reach the heights. So, accept the situation you have been handed. Do not let it weigh you down. You will have bad days, you will have terrible days, but you can get through them. You *will* get through them, and by doing so, you will give your child the best possible chance for a happier, brighter future.

Eventually you can look back and see what you have come through, and where you have been. When you do, I hope you will take a moment to pause and reflect, and say to yourself, "You know what? I really *am* a special mother."

Acknowledgments

There were so many special mothers who helped us with this book. We couldn't possibly have written it without their input. Their honesty, compassion, and advocacy formed the heart of our story.

Through our work together, they formed what we came to call the Special Mothers Club, something that probably would not have happened had we not all sat down to talk about the emotional side of LD and related issues. We are so grateful for their willingness to share their personal stories with us and with you. They are: Lisa, Janie, Dana, Helen, Marianne, Deborah, and our Special Father, John. We also thank Joyce, Tom, and Kristen for taking the time to share their thoughts with us.

Stephanie Thompson proved to be an invaluable resource: her insights and experiences inspired us in so many ways. Special thanks go to Sunny for being so upfront and courageous in discussing her life growing up with an LD sister.

The National Center for Learning Disabilities has worked hand in hand with us on this project right from the beginning. Their willingness to host the Web page component of *A Special Mother* will be of enormous benefit to our readers. It was a unique idea in the field of learning disabilities and allows this book and our readers to remain up to date on all the issues related to LD. We want to thank Executive Director James Wendorf, Laura Kaloi, Marcia Griffith, and two people who have guided us every step of the way, Marcelle White and, especially, Dr. Sheldon Horowitz.

Candace Cortiella, Director of the Advocacy Institute, is also author of NCLD's *IDEA Parent Guide*, which proved invaluable in our research.

We thank our agents, Phyllis Wender and Susie Cohen, and our publisher, Esther Margolis, and her amazing team at Newmarket Press: Keith Hollaman, Harry Burton, Heidi Sachner, and especially Linda Carbone.

Judy Woodruff, another special mother, is a very busy news broadcaster, but she graciously took time out from her schedule to write the wonderful Foreword. Thank you, Judy.

Thank you also to Allegra for being such an inspiration to me, and to all the mothers in our families: Charlotte, Kimm, Karen, and Stephanie.

Last, we thank our own mothers, Anne and Joan, and all mothers everywhere, especially those we hope will gain some measure of hope and comfort from this book.

Resources for Children with Learning Disabilities

NATIONAL ORGANIZATIONS

NATIONAL CENTER FOR LEARNING DISABILITIES (NCLD)

381 Park Avenue South, Suite 1401
New York, NY 10016
Telephone: 212-545-7510
Fax: 212-545-9665
Toll-Free: 888-575-7373
Web site: www.ld.org
A *Special Mother* webpage: www.ld.org/a-special-mother

NCLD provides essential information to parents, professionals, and individuals with learning disabilities, promotes research and programs to foster effective learning, and advocates for policies to protect and strengthen educational rights and opportunities.

Since its beginning, NCLD has been led by passionate and devoted parents committed to creating better outcomes for children, adolescents, and adults with learning disabilities. It provides national information and resources through its Web site.

NCLD has created a Web site component dedicated to the issues raised in this book (see link above).

INTERNATIONAL DYSLEXIA ASSOCIATION

40 York Road, 4th Floor
Baltimore, Maryland 21204
Telephone: 410-296-0232
Fax: 410-321-5069
Web site: www.interdys.org

International nonprofit membership organization that offers training in language programs and provides publications relating to dyslexia. Chapters are located in most states. The Association has 42 branches across the country that offer informational meetings and support groups. Referrals are made for persons seeking resources; in addition, the Association publishes journals and publications regarding dyslexia.

LD ONLINE
www.ldonline.org

Comprehensive online resource offering information on learning disabilities for parents and educators, as well as children and adults with learning disabilities. Features include basic and in-depth information, national events calendar, bulletin boards, audio clips from LD experts, and extensive resource listings with hyperlinks.

LEARNING DISABILITIES ASSOCIATION OF AMERICA (LDA)
4156 Library Road
Pittsburgh, PA 15234
Telephone: 412-341-1515
Fax: 412-344-0224
Web site: www.ldaamerica.org

National nonprofit membership organization, with state and local chapters, that conducts an annual conference and offers information and various publications. The LDA Web site contains a wealth of articles of interest to adults with LD and their parents. Call the national headquarters to receive a free information packet.

NATIONAL DISSEMINATION CENTER FOR CHILDREN WITH DISABILITIES (NICHCY)
1825 Connecticut Avenue NW, Suite 700
Washington, DC 20009
Telephone: 202-884-8200
Toll-Free: 800-695-0285
E-mail: nichcy@aed.org
Web site: www.nichcy.org

NICHCY is an information clearinghouse that provides free information on disabilities and related issues, focusing on children and youth (birth to age 25), including issues related to IDEA, the nation's Special Education law. Free services include personal responses, referrals, technical assistance, and information searches.

SMART KIDS WITH LEARNING DISABILITIES
38 Kings Highway North
Westport, CT 06880
Telephone: 203-226-6831
E-mail: Info@SmartKidswithLD.org
Web site: www.SmartKidswithLD.org

A nonprofit organization providing information, practical support, and encouragement to parents of children with learning disabilities and attention deficit disorders. Its national newsletter, Web site, and educational programs promote parents' critical role as advocates, while also highlighting the significant strengths of people with LD and ADHD.

WRIGHTSLAW
Web site: www.wrightslaw.com

The Wrightslaw mission is to provide parents, advocates, educators, and attorneys with accurate, up-to-date information about Special Education law and advocacy so they can be effective catalysts. You will find articles, cases, newsletters, and resources on dozens of topics in the Advocacy Libraries and Law Libraries. You may subscribe to *The Special Ed Advocate,* a free weekly e-newsletter about Special Education legal and advocacy topics. Of particular interest to parents looking for information about the *Individuals with Disabilities Education Act (IDEA).*

THE ADVOCACY INSTITUTE
Telephone: 540-364-0051.
E-mail: info@advocacyinstitute.org
Web site: www.advocacyinstitute.org

A nonprofit, tax-exempt organization dedicated to the development of products, projects, and services that work to improve the lives of people with disabilities. The Advocacy Institute provides consultative services to educators, counselors, service providers, organizations, government entities, and others. They cannot offer direct advocacy services to parents. Services can be individually designed to meet the unique needs of all those concerned with helping students with disabilities achieve their full potential. Their expert staff offers a wide range of knowledge and skills.

Index

About the Authors

Anne Ford served as Chairman of the Board of the National Center for Learning Disabilities (NCLD) from 1989 to 2001. During her term as Chair, she led the reorganization and broad expansion of NCLD, including establishing a presence in Washington, D.C., and organizing educational summits on learning disabilities in several regions of the United States. She has received many honors for her work in the field of learning disabilities, including the Lizette H. Sarnoff Award for Volunteer Service from the Albert Einstein College of Medicine. Leslie University has conferred upon her an Honorary Degree, Doctor of Humane Letters, for advocacy for people with learning disabilities.

Anne Ford is the author of the popular and inspirational book *Laughing Allegra*, about her experiences as the mother of a daughter with a learning disability, and *On Their Own: Creating an Independent Future for Your Adult Child with Learning Disabilities and ADHD*. She continues to work on behalf of people with LD, appearing as a keynote speaker at conferences and corporations, including JPMorgan Chase and Ford Motor Company.

John-Richard Thompson is an award-winning playwright and novelist living in New York City. He is co-author of Anne Ford's *Laughing Allegra* and *On Their Own*. His latest book is *The Christmas Mink*. For more information, visit his website www.j-rt.com.

Also by Anne Ford

LAUGHING ALLEGRA: The Inspiring Story of a Mother's Struggle and Triumph Raising a Daughter with Learning Disabilities

"Anne Ford shares the heartbreaking lows, the glorious highs, and lonely in-betweens of raising a daughter with a severe learning disability, at a time when few people, and few schools, knew what to do to help, or even tried."
—Judy Woodruff and Al Hunt

"This smart and welcome book is a gift for all parents, not just those with children with learning disabilities.... An insightful guide through the challenges and rewards of parenting." —Tom Brokaw

"This poignant, intimate portrait opens an often hidden world and illuminates the many ways learning disabilities shape the lives of entire families."
—*Publishers Weekly*

ON THEIR OWN: Creating an Independent Future for Your Adult Child with Learning Disabilities and ADHD

"With a deep understanding of the worries that are universal to parents of children with disabilities, Anne Ford has managed to provide down-to-earth, practical advice on every area that affects an adult child's future and ability to live independently: school, work, social life, financial well-being." —Sally Shaywitz, M.D., author of *Overcoming Dyslexia*

"With insight, candor, and optimism, this is a remarkably helpful book for parents and families who are dealing with the impact of learning disabilities as their children move up and out." —James Wendorf, Executive Director, National Center for Learning Disabilities

---

LAUGHING ALLEGRA by Anne Ford with John-Richard Thompson
272 pages. 6" x 9". 22 photos. Includes answers to most commonly asked questions, legal rights, resource guide, index. Foreword by Mel Levine, M.D.
ISBN: 978-1-55704-622-2. $16.95. pb. • 978-1-55704-564-5. $24.95. hc.

ON THEIR OWN by Anne Ford with John-Richard Thompson
320 pages. 6" x 9". Foreword by Sally Shaywitz.
ISBN: 978-1-55704-725-0. $16.95. pb. • 978-1-55704-759-5. $24.95. hc.

Our books are available from your local bookseller or from Newmarket Press, 18 East 48th Street, New York, NY 10017; phone 212-832-3575 or 800-669-3903; fax 212-832-3629; e-mail info@newmarketpress.com. Prices and availability are subject to change. Catalogs and information on quantity order discounts are available upon request.

www.newmarketpress.com

www.laughingallegra.com
www.ld.org/aspecialmother